THE RENAISSANCE OF ASIA

THE RENAISSANCE OF ASIA

LECTURES DELIVERED UNDER THE AUSPICES OF
THE COMMITTEE ON INTERNATIONAL RELATIONS
ON THE LOS ANGELES CAMPUS OF
THE UNIVERSITY OF CALIFORNIA
1939

UNIVERSITY OF CALIFORNIA PRESS
BERKELEY AND LOS ANGELES
1941

UNIVERSITY OF CALIFORNIA PRESS
BERKELEY, CALIFORNIA

CAMBRIDGE UNIVERSITY PRESS
LONDON, ENGLAND

COPYRIGHT, 1941, BY THE
REGENTS OF THE UNIVERSITY OF CALIFORNIA

PREFACE

THE LECTURES in the pages which follow were delivered on the Los Angeles campus of the University in the spring of 1939. Planned by the Committee on International Relations with a view to bringing to student attention, well ahead of the development of acute crisis, the basic problems of the whole Asiatic continent, they have more than justified the Committee's hopes and expectations. The Committee regrets that, through circumstances beyond its control, it proved impossible to include in the 1939 series, as an initiation into the mysteries of Levantine politics, an inaugural lecture on Egypt, Iraq, and Iran. This lacuna is the more regrettable because the treatment of Arab and Iranian nationalism would have contributed much toward the understanding of a region which, no less than Chungking, Kunming, or Singapore, is at the forefront of strategy and politics in the Near East. As this volume is the definitive record of lectures actually delivered, rather than a compilation *ad hoc,* the book is issued in the full consciousness that its scope is unfortunately curtailed. Notwithstanding this difficulty, the lectures are now offered to a wider public, in the political climate of 1941, essentially in the form in which they were delivered. To compensate for various delays in publication, the individual authors were given ample opportunity, in the spring of this year, to revise their manuscripts. Few indeed were the changes! This fact attests, not the obstinacy of professors in clinging to petrified viewpoints, but the clarity of their perception and perspective, which intervening events have only served to confirm. Because the manuscripts themselves evidence the high accuracy of the original analyses of the problems treated, the Committee on International Relations takes peculiar pride in presenting the finished offering to the public at this time.

At the moment of writing, events have not as yet brought India into the actual arena of hostilities. Nevertheless, India remains a tremendous factor in the deciding of the way along which the future of civilization will travel. The careful survey of India's internal problems, of her complex social and institutional structure, given by Professor Klingberg brings into clear relief the role which India is predestined to play in the evolution of Asia. To disclose the basic pattern of Indian nationalism and show its vitality and congruity with the behavior of comparable movements elsewhere in Asia; to depict the impending convergence of the forces of aggressive imperialism in southeastern Asia and the Middle East; to forecast so candidly the eventual emergence of latent trends in Indian polity; to reveal, well in advance of war, the formula of crisis behavior on the part of India—this is surely no mean accomplishment in such small compass; it attests to perspicacity of a very high order.

Indo-China has been less fortunate than India: her territory has suffered a dual invasion, and she has undergone a partition ill concealed by the smokescreen of Japanese mediation. In the Treaty of Tokio and its three annexed protocols of May 9, 1941, are found the terms of the "settlement" that has validated the claims of Thailand and given material satisfaction to Japan. How weak the territorial structure, how

Preface vii

frail and precarious the hold of France on Indo-China proved to be, occasion no surprise to the reader of Professor Knight's discussion. Here are depicted with clear and uncanny foresight the unsubstantial character of French colonial control and the ineluctable consequences of an impossible policy of autarchy-at-long-range. Professor Knight seems to have realized in advance, as did few of his countrymen, how sorry would be the role which Indo-China would inevitably play in the impending tragedy. Behind the imposing façade of publicized French activity he has found in reality little of constructive achievement. In the halcyon days from 1934 to 1939 it was not easy to be frankly skeptical and doubting, but events have confirmed to an astonishing degree, and so made particularly timely, Professor Knight's diagnosis and prognosis of Indo-China's ills.

At a time when the visible, terrifying, mechanized war machines seem to be the prime movers in civilization, when, to use Mussolini's favorite phrase, "it is blood that moves the wheels of history," it is extremely valuable to have the inner workings, the invisible mechanics and hidden dynamics of power, exposed to the public view. This Dr. Kawai has done with high fidelity and extreme precision in his analysis of the working forces involved in the ever-shifting struggle for power behind the throne in Japanese politics. American readers, whether they be student or lay, will find the dynamisms in Japanese political life that ended the golden glow of the "Shidehara decade" (which, incidentally, coincided with our own "gilded decade") convincingly portrayed and realistically treated. It is clear that the "new order" which has now been vouchsafed a decade in which to intrench itself in Greater East Asia will not easily let go, and that considerably more than the one-time magic abracadabra of phrases, as found, let us say, in the Washington treaties of 1921-22, will be required to dislodge it. But Dr. Kawai has done more than reveal deep anchorages and inward strains; he has furnished a number of clues to the internal play of Japanese politics and done much to explain why continuing crises are perennially settled by "impossible" compromises which produce in turn an Ugaki, a Nomura, a Konoye as the dominant spirits in the shifting, short-lived coalitions which successively govern Japan.

Treating an altogether different aspect of the Far Eastern problem from the standpoint of one not only intimately conversant with the aspirations of Chinese nationalism, but deeply grounded in the history of Japanese territorial expansion, Professor Mah, in his treatment of Sino-Japanese relations, follows worthily in the tradition and the fine line of high scholarship of the late Professor Yoshi S. Kuno. Sedulously buttressing his interpretations of events from the highest impartial sources, Dr. Mah presents his views with conviction and with a wealth of irrefutable authority. These are not the musings of effervescent and romantic Chinese nationalism; here, of a verity, is the quintessence of objective scholarship and balanced interpretation.

No treatment of the vast new life that has been surging through Asia in the years since the First World War would be complete without an overview of that tremendous stretch of territory—Asiatic Russia—for which war and revolution

Preface ix

opened up unexpected and far-reaching social change. Thus the survey of Soviet Russia and Asia by Professor Kerner fittingly links the developments in the Levant with those in the Middle and Far East. With sharp strokes he depicts the continuity of a long historical process and the violent breaks with the traditional pattern. He sets in juxtaposition the "religious political imperialism" of the Tsars and the "mystical social imperialism" of the Bolsheviks, only to find that they are analogous significant dynamisms of two assertedly antithetical regimes which paradoxically operate in a strangely parallel fashion! Soviet policy was indeed at the crossroads on the very day when Professor Kerner delivered his lecture. While he hoped for an evolution of Soviet foreign policy which would strengthen the system of collective security then so sadly in need of reënforcement, he was not oblivious of the other alternative, involving "some measure of accommodation with both Japan and Germany"—witness the Soviet-German pact of August 23, 1939, and that between the U.S.S.R. and Japan on April 6, 1941—to which the equivocal policies of the "nonaggressors," as Stalin so contemptuously called them, conduced. Indeed, one has but to substitute the word "Axis" for "Anti-Comintern" in the text, as has already been done in the strange play of politics, to see that the idea of "an agreement to distribute territories and sources of raw materials on a world-wide scale . . . by a close coördination of aggressive moves in various parts of the world" was implicit in the world situation of May, 1939; that it has become a concrete reality the stirring events in Iraq and Syria, indicative of Soviet participation in the redistribution of that quarter of the world, are already witness today.

Preface

In dealing with "The Future of China" Professor Steiner brings into vivid relief his impressions of the vigor and capacity for resistance of the Chinese as he actually observed these qualities in their midst. Fearlessly he paints a picture of renascent China "standing up in her shaken depths" and exhibiting magnificent qualities of endurance which, with the passing months, continue to call forth American admiration. In making, in 1939, so strong a statement as that "unless she forges strong ties with powerful allies, she [Japan] has no chance for ultimate victory in whole or in part," Dr. Steiner knowingly incurred a great risk, yet his candid conviction with respect to the long-run victory of the Chinese merely anticipated by a biennium the confident and unequivocal pronouncement of Generalissimo Chiang Kai-shek on May 12, 1941, to the effect that China, even if given only material and economic aid, can defeat Japan single-handed—so great has been the reserve of Chinese resistance and so great the exhaustion of Japan. In Dr. Steiner's pages basic knowledge and conversant interpretation have combined to bring unusual perspicacity and precision.

Whether the Renaissance of Asia will end in a redistribution of power among the strong in that continent and in Europe, or will lead to a definitive establishment of national rights among the nascent peoples, rests, in the last analysis, upon the power of resistance of Britain, China, and their allies to the outthrust of totalitarian power toward Asia.

May 15, 1941.

MALBONE W. GRAHAM

CONTENTS

	PAGE
India under the New Constitution	3
By FRANK J. KLINGBERG, Professor of History	
The Role of Indo-China in Asia	37
By MELVIN M. KNIGHT, Professor of Economics	
Domestic Factors in Japanese Foreign Policy . . .	63
By KAZUO KAWAI, Instructor in History	
Japan's Aims and Aspirations on the Continent of Asia	93
By N. WING MAH, Associate Professor of Political Science	
Soviet Russia in Asia	121
By ROBERT J. KERNER, Professor of Modern European History	
The Future of China	145
By H. ARTHUR STEINER, Assistant Professor of Political Science	

INDIA UNDER THE
NEW CONSTITUTION

FRANK J. KLINGBERG
PROFESSOR OF HISTORY
IN THE UNIVERSITY OF CALIFORNIA

Lecture delivered April 3, 1939

INDIA UNDER THE NEW CONSTITUTION

THE PURPOSE of this series of lectures about Asia in renaissance is to examine the cause, impetus, and course of nationalism in the several countries of that vast continent, and my assignment is to explore the particularly significant developments which are uniting India while it is still under the supervision of the British. The British, on their part, are endeavoring to achieve through a wholesale transfer of their rich and many-sided experiences a constitutional solution, not in this case for a new country such as Canada and Australia, but for the most ancient of peoples, so that East and West, contrary to Kipling, are deeply involved in a common enterprise.

Instead of presenting a somewhat specialized paper related to my own particular interest, that of British humanitarianism in the 18th and 19th centuries as it ameliorated exploitation of native races, I shall attempt in this introductory lecture to present a survey of those features of British expansion into Asia which have contributed to the renaissance of Asia, and I shall outline the revival of one world-significant center of nationalism, namely, India.

A sustained effort is now being made to recognize the emerging nationalism of this subcontinent of nearly 2,000,000 square miles, with its teeming millions of people, by the grant of a new constitution of great scope and complexity, its main text 431 pages long.[1] The intricate provisions of this document

[1] *Government Of India Act, 1935;* 25 and 26 Geo. 5, ch. 42, pp. xxiv, 1–431. The literature of India, even in English, is far too vast for any one reader to

4   *The Renaissance of Asia*

of the year 1935 give at least some hint of the appalling difficulties of the Indian question. A brief historical statement will perhaps help to clarify the problems.

In outbursts of nationalistic fervor, such as that of many-voiced India, it is to be noted that each people, in periods of self-consciousness, recovers a view of its past, recalls its early heroes, its legends, and the fabulous achievements of ancient times. One might say that, while building a future, a nation in the process of renaissance creates also a glorious past, and that for each brick laid for the future a brick is added to the temple of past greatness.

Of India's great age and genuine heritage an eminent writer, Sir Valentine Chirol, member of the Royal Commission in the Indian Public Service, has significantly said: "The Aryan peoples, who may be recognized as the first foreign conquerors of India, laid the foundations of Indian civilization long before Rome or Athens was born and longer still before the rest of Europe emerged from savagery, and unlike any of the ancient civilizations of the world, excepting pos-

---

record his own years of reading. New books about present-day conditions appear in numbers: for example, C. F. Andrews, *True India;* C. F. Andrews and Girija Mookerjee, *The Rise of the Congress Movement;* Leonard M. Schiff, *The Present Condition of India;* N. Gangulee, *Health and Nutrition in India.* These books are reviewed in *The Listener,* March 2 and March 16, 1939.

The Cambridge History of India supplies a comprehensive coöperative account from ancient times to 1918. Vol. 2 has not yet appeared. Through the kindness of Captain Angus Fletcher, of the British Library of Information, the writer had access to some material of special interest. See also Arthur Berriedale Keith, *A Constitutional History of India, 1600–1935* (London, Methuen and Co., 1936); [British] Foreign Office, *The Constitutions of All Countries— The British Empire* (London, His Majesty's Stationery Office, 1938).

Klingberg: India 5

sibly the Chinese, it has remained a living civilization."[2] He reminds us that this ancient India, steeped in its own traditions, was already 3000 years old before the first English merchant-adventurer stood upon Indian soil, a forerunner of what became the superimposition of Western culture upon the wide area of India. The period of Robert Clive and Warren Hastings and of the American Revolution, 150 to 200 years ago, is therefore but a most recent page in the history of India.

The American Revolution did not destroy the British Empire, but it did make it predominantly Asiatic. Besides, it determined that of the 500 million people in the Empire today, 425 million are black men or brown men, leaving a body of 75 million people of European origin in Great Britain and the self-governing Dominions. Of the 425 million non-Europeans, 350 millions—nearly one-fifth of the world's population—are in India, thousands of miles away from London, the center of empire authority. The conquest and government of India, therefore, furnish the most startling illustration of empire building in modern times.

Perhaps the nature of the British conquest of India, in the 18th and 19th centuries, can be understood only in the light of a number of concurrent revolutions in Great Britain, which so intensified British strength that all European rivals were

[2] *India* (New York, Charles Scribner's Sons, 1932), p. 1. This authoritative work is the most illuminating book available, even though it was finished in 1925. Another penetrating work is that of Hans Kohn, *A History of Nationalism in the East* (New York, Harcourt, Brace and Company, 1929). See also Sir Francis Younghusband, *Dawn in India, British Purpose and Indian Aspiration* (London, John Murray, 1930).

6 *The Renaissance of Asia*

pushed aside. The industrial revolution, the agricultural revolution, the revolutionary increases in population, added to supremacy in commerce, created a British state many times more powerful than that of a few short decades before at the opening of the 18th century. Recently an American engineer stated that an American, aided by machinery, was equal to thirty or forty Chinamen in his economic strength—and the first modern industrial state, namely Great Britain, is the prime illustration of European mastery of the forces of nature by means of scientific investigation, multiple invention, genius for organization, capacity for military and naval fighting, and a love of adventure and of colonization which in sum total created the mood of "manifest destiny," later eloquently stated by Kipling, poet of imperialism.

As set forth by Lillian Knowles, "The British Empire has been mainly founded by traders organized in companies.... Thus the most important parts and the larger continental areas of the British tropics are a result of company trading, and the British Tropics are in origin a trader's Empire."[3] This fact of joint stock company origin naturally meant that only a relatively small number of citizens were interested in any one company, and accounts for Professor Seeley's statement: "We seem, as it were, to have conquered and peopled half the world in a fit of absence of mind."[4] Individual initiative in foreign trade, in emigration, and even in faraway administra-

---
[3] *The Economic Development of the British Overseas Empire* (London, George Routledge and Sons, 1924), pp. 261–262.

[4] Quoted from Sir John R. Seeley, *The Expansion of England*, by Lord Lytton in *The Listener*, p. 379, February 16, 1939. The statement appears in Seeley (London, The Macmillan Company, 1883), p. 8.

tion have been outstanding characteristics of British empire building.

Under these conditions, only a relatively few Englishmen, the stockholders and Parliamentary committees, knew the full history of a new trading enterprise in a distant part of the world. British humanitarian effort, therefore, has had for its purpose the exposing of the concealed iniquities of the trader, whether he was a slave trader on the Atlantic or an unscrupulous businessman in India.

In the decades after Waterloo, a world map which showed the British Empire in red would be totally misleading to the modern eye because the Empire in its economic overlordship still included the United States, Latin America, and a good part of the continent of Europe. And besides, it extended through the Mediterranean and held in economic vassalage in greater or less degree the Turkish Empire, Persia, India, Australasia, and China. In short, trade had far outrun the flag, and among the junior partners were the fabulously rich Dutch East Indies, which Great Britain had perhaps inadvertently returned to Holland after Napoleon's defeat. The British conqueror of Java, Sir Stamford Raffles, founded the city of Singapore at this time.

Eminent also among the junior partners was the Sultan of Turkey, who as caliph of the Mohammedan world had tremendous influence in northern Africa, Arabia, Persia, and among the tens of millions of Mohammedans in India and in the Dutch East Indies. Obviously, under these circumstances the bad man was the Russian, who was variously characterized in the contemporary phrases of propaganda as "the bear who walks like a man," "scratch a Russian and you get a Tartar." In fact, occasionally, Great Britain, amply aided by allies, fought or nearly fought, in wars such as the Crimean, the Russo-Turkish, the Russo-Japanese, against this Russian, who was regarded as a primary threat against the whole Eurasian-British empire. If the 18th century was the age in which France was regarded as the primary enemy of British dominion, in much of the 19th Russia either took first place or was added to France as a virile enemy power.

Always strikingly enlightening to an American is a visit to Westminster Abbey, where just place is given to those statesmen, admirals, and generals who in the 18th and 19th centuries held French and Russian power in check. Perhaps the greatest of them all was Stratford de Redcliffe, ambassador to St. Petersburg and later to Constantinople, and always an Empire outpost or chief watchdog of Russian moves. In the years before the Great War, as is well known, Russia became a member of the Triple Entente and fought against the Central Powers.

Curiously enough, while the primary aim of military and naval measures was the protection of British interests in India from European rivals, the idea that India might herself rise and drive out her European conquerors was only dimly envisioned by Russians in Siberia, French in Indo-China, Spaniards in the Philippines, Dutch in the Spice Islands, or British rulers in India. The onrush of the West with its industrial and commercial skills, its faith in progress, its military power, its many-sided capacity in the arts and sciences, its missionary zeal, seemed clearly to foreshadow the early Euro-

Klingberg: India

peanization of the whole world, with a future Indian people who would be Englishmen with dark skins, as described in 1835 in Macaulay's famous Minute on Education. A superimposed English language and British culture, with the Indian civilizations receding rapidly into the limbo of a dimly remembered past, was the dream and program of the 19th-century administrators.

Railroads, canals, telegraphs, roads and bridges, medicine and sanitation, Christianity with its spirit of mastery over all human and natural forces, were imported and were to speed Hindu and Mohammedan quickly into the white man's golden age of universal progress.

The following thumbnail sketch of India is a striking instance of Macaulay's rare brevity: "The task of the English, when they assumed control was, according to Macaulay, 'to reconstruct a decayed society.' Above all it had to try and protect the peasant and raise his standard of life. The British took over India in a state of economic nakedness. There were no metalled roads, docks, harbours, canals, hospitals, schools, colleges, printing presses, or other requirements of Western civilized life, and neither the disposition nor the means on the part of the population to provide them. The canals had dried up and enormous areas of land were sheer waste. British rule had to play the part of a universal provider and special providence, and India is the great example of what a Government can effect in raising the economic standard of a country."[5]

The first rude resistance to this European inroad in India

---
[5] Knowles, *op. cit.*, p. 274.

occurred at the time of the mutiny of 1857, which today is being reinterpreted as the first blow struck by Hindu and Mohammedan for Indian nationalism and Indian home rule, if not complete independence.

A few comments on the success of Westernization may be illuminating in view of the rapid progress of nationalism. Most Americans have read Macaulay the historian, but are unaware of his four-year administrative career in India, where he decided a bitterly fought educational controversy in favor of Western education in the English language in his Minute of February 2, 1835. In the Minute he greatly undervalued the spiritual power of the ancient civilizations of India, but nevertheless convinced leading Hindus that they must turn to the West for a new inspiration. These Indians founded colleges of their own, such as the Hindu College in Calcutta, and some of them became Christians. They carried the tide of Western education into all the chief centers of India before 1850. The great administrators of the period, Sir Thomas Munro, Lord William Bentinck, Lord Dalhousie, threw their weight in favor of the spread of Western culture. British educational and missionary pioneers either could not foresee that they were forging a weapon for eventual self-government, or else they welcomed this possibility. Macaulay, indeed, predicted, as already stated, that in a few generations there would be nothing to distinguish an educated Indian from an Englishman except his dark complexion. If Western language, Western education, Western law should result in creating a self-governing nation, Lord Macaulay thought England's mission in India would be ended.

Klingberg: India

Macaulay was merely one of the men of his time who devoted themselves to land, judicial, and other reforms for the people of India. Alexander Duff founded the great Medical School at Calcutta in 1835. About the same time, a well-known decree stopped the burning of widows. Throughout the first half of the 19th century, color feeling at least was singularly absent from the program of British administrators because they were still under the influence of the cult of the "noble savage," the evangelical fervor of Christian brotherhood, and the stimulus to justice from the indictment of Warren Hastings by Edmund Burke. Moreover, the Westernization was taking place at the top, and these administrators respected many of the customs of the people and gave a new sense of security to the humblest folk of the Peninsula. While it is true that Macaulay had a very inadequate appreciation of Oriental literature, it is also true that other eminent Britons studied this literature, edited it, translated it into English, produced Sanskrit grammars, and founded chairs of Sanskrit, calling to their aid German and French scholars, among them the world-renowned Max Müller. By this process they revealed to India a grandeur in her past which she herself had only dimly suspected.

A constant scrutiny of the affairs of the East India Company, especially at the frequent times of renewal of the charter, kept alive the idea of trusteeship which had been so fiercely implanted by Burke. For example, Parliament in 1833, more than 100 years ago, emphatically declared that "no native of the said Indian territories shall by reason only of his religion, place of birth, descent, color, or any of them be

The Renaissance of Asia

disabled from holding any place, office, or employment under the Company." Furthermore, the largest possible number of Indians was to be employed in administrative work. Just before the mutiny of 1857 a scheme for education of the lower classes was being formulated. Governor Dalhousie particularly took pride in his educational achievements and in material progress such as the building of railways and telegraphs.

When India became crown territory after the Mutiny, by royal proclamation in 1858, the idea of educating and using Indians in the government of India was reiterated, as it was many times afterward, anticipating the steps toward dominion status which have been undertaken since the Great War.

With the development of the facilities for travel, many Indians went to the English universities and were even welcomed in English society. These travelers and observers, who witnessed the unification of Italy and Germany, and the emergence of Japan, began to dream of an Indian nation, and in 1885 gave the first concrete evidence of their plans in the Indian National Congress—which has met regularly since. The chief demand at first was for a larger participation in the public services, a demand which was supported by some of the English in India. This first small body of 100 delegates, from all parts of India, was the beginning of the movement which now has the attention of the world, and which has repeatedly shaken India to its foundations.

British success in conquering, governing, and superimposing first the veneer, and then more of the substance, of Western culture upon India is due in part to the fact that during the 18th and the first half of the 19th centuries both Mohammedanism and Hinduism were at a low ebb. Neither Mohammedan nor Hindu could dispute in terms of intellectual equality with either the British scholar or the Westernized Indian. In the years immediately preceding the meeting of the first National Congress, Hindu pioneers, foreshadowing Gandhi, and occasionally Mohammedan leaders, began to rise upon the scene, and the wave of anti-Western reaction began. Indian thinkers and observers visited the United States and England to promulgate their own faiths and gained recruits in the Western world. Instead of coöperating with the British leaders, they denounced their fellows who were coöperating as satellites, slaves, and enemies of India. Instead of being apologetic for their own views, they became aggressive and defended all Hindu customs, including even child marriage. Students of the West, as they often were, they were learning its political obstructionist tactics from Irish nationalists. Slowly the Indian National Congress reflected these tendencies.

The heavy taxation, large military expenditures, grievances, petty and great, together with demands for primary education, became an annual complaint. British officials viewed this outburst as a safety valve for intellectuals and unemployed lawyers, not realizing then—what we now know so well from recent European events—that with undercurrents of widespread grievance a few determined men can revolutionize a people, found a nationalism, and establish a modern state. In one striking instance of the renaissance of Asia the motive power was supplied by the leaders of the country without being conquered by foreigners, namely, in Japan; in India, on the other hand, rebirth has developed under the overlordship of Great Britain. In India, after the mid-19th century, great religious revivals in Hinduism and in Mohammedanism occurred, and by 1885 these revivals marched side by side with the Congress movement and showed a spirit of revolt against Western domination. British rulers were aware of their own success in furnishing India with many of the scientific and technical appliances of the Western world, and in covering the land with highways, railroads, telegraph lines, irrigation projects, medical foundations, and schools, and at times resented the ingratitude of the Indian nationalist leaders.

By the opening of the 20th century it had become obvious to careful observers that the peoples of India, while accepting many of the Western improvements, were nevertheless determined to maintain the essentials of their own ancient civilizations. The railways, welcomed by all the pilgrims, were used as a new means of reaching their shrines and temples. All these mechanical appliances and the study of a common language did not necessarily bind the people to England, but gave them a means of communication with each other as they struggled for greater recognition and independence. Medical care, again, a gift of the English, prevented some of the losses of population, so that the increase, now 5 millions a year,[8] was not checked by disease and famine. The labors of scholarship helped to create the glorious past, a necessary part of the fervor of nationalism. The Boer War of 1899-1902 showed

---
[8] "India's Food Problem," *The Listener*, Suppl. 4, March 16, 1939. Fifty millions were added to the population between 1921 and 1931, and a further, perhaps even greater, increase is in prospect.

that British power was not invulnerable; the Russo-Japanese War of 1904-1905, that Oriental peoples could act on terms of equality with European nations.

Moreover, during the 18th and 19th centuries it was possible for the Europeans to carry on civil wars in Europe and to build empires in other countries at the same time; the non-European world was incapable of resisting, even in a small degree, the penetrating powers of European invasions. On Queen Victoria's sixtieth jubilee in 1897, Japan alone seemed destined to resist the Europeanization of the whole world. Europeans, although they realized increasingly that the non-European world was in revolt, and wrote books on the conflict of color, the menace of color, and the like, were not able in 1914, nor later, to present a common European front to the emerging nationalisms of the East. Japan, for its part, was given a permanent seat on the Council of the League of Nations and was repeatedly recognized as one of the great powers, capable perhaps of repeating in Asia what Europeans had succeeded in doing in their conquests in Asia and in Africa. Indeed, shrewd but generous Japanese statesmen lamented during the Great War that such slaughter and continual civil war in Europe would spell the decline of the West and cause its relapse into barbarism.

With Europe crippled by the Great War, the murmurs of a new Asiatic order could be heard increasingly from China and India. In the latter country Gandhi appeared as the man of destiny, arousing the people in favor of the ancient religious forces; and, standing forth as an opponent of Western invasion in all its forms, he fought for home rule. Already famous for his defense of the Hindus in South Africa, he had by that activity stamped himself as the leader of the Hindus against discrimination in all parts of the world. He had vigorously supported the British in the Boer War, raising an Indian Ambulance Field Corps and leading it to the front, because he was convinced that the establishment of British supremacy in South Africa would right the wrongs of the Hindus. To his chagrin he found that South Africa under the British flag checked Indian immigration and imposed additional racial disabilities. He developed his South African policy of passive resistance with hunger strikes and mass demonstrations, still convinced that the British sense of justice would not permit a discrimination against the expansion of India, which for almost 100 years had been sending its people into the East Indies, the West Indies, the Mauritius, South Africa, Canada, and the United States, and in so great a degree that India herself was becoming a mother land with colonies over the world. The viceroy of India, at Madras, November 24, 1913, expressed "the sympathy of India, deep and burning, and not only of India, but of all lovers of India like myself, for their compatriots in South Africa in their resistance to invidious and unjust laws."[7]

Aided from Whitehall, and by the government of India, Gandhi was able to gain some concessions for the Indians in South Africa, a conciliatory gesture effective for the length of the Great War. Not only had Indian troops fought side by side with British regiments on European battlefields, but India had been admitted on equal footing with the Domin-

---
[7] Sir Valentine Chirol, *op. cit.*, p. 202.

Klingberg: India 17

ions to the Imperial War Councils in London, and to the Peace Conference in Paris, and had been made an original member of the League of Nations. India, of course, was still really represented by Britons rather than by Indians.

India seemed on the road to full Empire membership; it was promised such a position in the British Commonwealth of Nations. Gandhi himself in the Great War, as in the Boer War, threw his weight on the side of British victory, and was in large part responsible for the tremendous Indian effort. By way of illustration, in March, 1918, at the time of the great crisis on the western front, he asked for and got from one small district a contingent of 12,000 troops.[8] He envisioned India as a full partner in the Empire and believed allied victory would give her that position. He admired Englishmen and hoped they would abandon their pride of race and love of power. But his South African miniature campaign was never absent from his mind as a possible weapon in India, and as a student of Tolstoi he had come to suspect authority as the source of all evil.

Under these postwar conditions any serious clash in India was dangerous because the Gandhi weapon of noncoöperation could be called into action. At this moment, shortly after the Great War, terroristic bands, as often before, were suppressed as criminal conspiracies by the Indian Government, which was invested with special police powers. This particular suppression caused Gandhi to proclaim passive resistance, which he called civil resistance or noncoöperation, a treatment of the government as no less untouchable than the

[8] *Ibid.*, p. 203.

The Renaissance of Asia

lowest castes of Hinduism. Only under Hinduism, with its caste system, could so unusual an attack be used successfully. Naturally, such a campaign would ordinarily have no appeal to the 80 million Mohammedans, whose religious conceptions are strikingly different from those of the Hindus. But the Mohammedans, in turn, had been seriously offended by the defeat of Turkey and the destruction of the caliphate at Constantinople. And, in addition, a common bond was the attraction of the ascetic saintliness of Gandhi. He was careful to make no distinction between Hindu and Mohammedan, with the result that thousands of both religions flocked to hear him. He campaigned to free the untouchables from their position. His frailty, asceticism, and personal magnetism gave him a hold over the silent masses which was difficult, if not impossible, for Westerners to understand.

Mohammedanism, with its democratic, militant, rigid, monotheistic creed, stands in sharp contrast with caste-ridden and yet flexible, philosophical, and polytheistic Hinduism. Hinduism, ever in motion, has had the elasticity from time immemorial to absorb other faiths and to produce recently such men as Tagore the poet, Singh the Christian mystic, Radhakrishnan the philosopher, and Gandhi the nationalistic leader.

Gandhi has been committed throughout to a program of nonviolence, but it was not to be expected that the millions of his followers could avoid bloodshed. On April 6, 1919, a collision occurred in Delhi, followed some time later by mob attacks at Amritsar, of unholy memory, in which five Englishmen were killed. The mobs were suppressed before General Dyer arrived upon the scene, but, finding a protest meeting of 6000 to 10,000 people assembled in a small enclosure, he opened fire without warning with machine guns, killed 379, wounded 1200, to whom no aid was given, and issued a crawling order (requiring Indians to walk on all fours in a certain street), which later was withdrawn by the lieutenant governor. But Indian opinion was completely inflamed long before the machinery of the British Government officially condemned General Dyer for his action. Gandhi did repeated penance for the violences committed by his followers, but, on the other hand, denounced the government as satanic, and henceforth worked for united action by Mohammedan and Hindu.

More specifically, Gandhi boycotted the 1919 Government of India Act by asking that no Indians vote or stand as candidates for the Legislative Councils and that no Indian import or use British manufactures; all were to wear homespun clothes of native-grown cotton. All Indians were to resign their offices, give up their titles, withdraw from their professions, take their children from the schools, and, later on, refuse to pay taxes. By this exercise of "soul force" would India attain self-government within a year, in Gandhi's expectation. His plan was only partly successful, but he became the idol of the masses in a way unexampled since the days of Buddha. He constantly talked of the beauty and freedom of village life in the olden days, and although he condemned violence it was carried on in his name. The Gandhi movement was particularly hostile to Western industrialism, and strikes were common, the people smashing liquor shops, then

20 *The Renaissance of Asia*

teapots, as symbols of Western influence. Racial hatred naturally developed rapidly.

Concurrently with Gandhi's leadership of the Hindus was a Mohammedan Caliphate movement in which an attempt was made, again shortly after the Great War, to convince the 80 million Mohammedans in India that the defeat of the sultan was an attack upon Islam. The result was that the old Mohammedan confidence in British rule was seriously undermined. Two brothers, Mohammed and Shaukat Ali, prisoners during the Great War, led delegations to see David Lloyd George and received sympathy in Great Britain, especially from the Jews, who had not forgotten that the Mohammedan Turk had provided a city of refuge for them when they were driven out of Spain. Gandhi and the brothers Ali joined forces in the movement for self-government, a significant moment for the new Hindu-Mohammedan coöperation. Extremely dangerous to British rule this coöperation might have become, had not the Angora Assembly, at this very moment, abolished the Caliphate.

Under these strained relations the Government of India Act of 1919 was proclaimed on February 9, 1921. The proclamation from the king-emperor stated: "Today you have the beginnings of 'Swaraj' (self-government) within my Empire and the widest scope and ample opportunity for progress to the liberty which my other dominions enjoy." Briefly, the constitution provided for a substantial grant of power to Indians for a ten-year stage, with the proviso that within this time a full investigation into the working of this experiment would be undertaken. The grant of powers to the Indians with reservations was known as dyarchy (double authority, giving powers to the Indians and reserving powers to the old government). This particular constitution inevitably was full of most amazing details. It granted provincial powers to big blocks of territory, but it did not materially change the central setup of administration and legislation, and it did not affect the Indian native princes. About one-third of India is still ruled by the native princes, with British advice. The intricate provisions were admittedly for a period of transition, and this constitution can therefore be described as an installment of responsible self-government in the provinces. In the limited space here available it is impossible to develop the details, of representation, election, suffrage, reserved powers, and the like. One fact may, however, be mentioned: $5\frac{1}{2}$ million voters, or about 3 per cent of a total of 240 million British Indians, excluding native states, were placed on the rolls, a number increased to 14 per cent in the Constitution of 1935. Both sexes may now vote. Side by side with this constitution there was a determined effort to turn the administrative services over more largely to the Indians. Oddly enough, the total number of Englishmen holding important positions in these services was only about 6000. This declaration of future policy had the strange effect of discouraging preparation for the civil services in England, in that it was prophetic of the future developments of a career service primarily for Indians themselves.

With the elections boycotted by Gandhi, the more conservative candidates were chosen to the legislative bodies. The legislative assembly began work in February, 1921, under conditions of considerable mutual forbearance, despite the Amritsar tragedy. The Prince of Wales visited India at this time, a boycott was declared against him by Gandhi, and serious outrages occurred in Bombay on the day of his landing. This 1921 visit was made in Lord Reading's first year of viceroyalty and at a time of Gandhi's highest prestige.

In 1924 a new, more violent, Swarajist self-government party, under the leadership of C. R. Das, Gandhi's lieutenant in Bengal, captured most of the legislative machinery of India, especially the legislative assembly, and forced the viceroy to use his emergency powers. Gandhi had been temporarily shoved aside and there was now keener legislative manipulation and less talk about "soul force." Gandhi was willing to forget and forgive, but the new party wished the British driven out relentlessly. The turning over of the civil services to Indians, the Indianization of the army, fiscal autonomy, and a protective tariff were objectives kept to the fore by this new and vigorous party, almost as skillful in destruction as the House of Commons usually is in constructive legislation. However, at the very moment when success seemed to be on the horizon, the old and bitter feud between Hindu and Mohammedan, over the question of which should dominate India, broke out afresh. The old All-India Moslem League was revived and met independently from the largely Hindu National Congress. If India was to be governed by and for its people, the division of the spoils was already a matter of negotiations between the two parties.

And this summary of the situation in 1924 and 1925 brings us to the Constitution of 1935. This exceedingly complicated act with its 478 sections, running in length to 431 quarto pages, including 16 schedules, cannot of course be discussed in detail in this analysis.

A brief constitutional survey of the thirty years from 1909 to 1939 may be helpful at this point. The fundamental policy of Great Britain during the last thirty years has been one of gradualism—self-government to be applied first locally and then nationally,—a policy which has called for great patience on the part of the people of India. The Morley-Minto reforms of 1909 had introduced the electoral principle into the Indian legislature and somewhat widened its sphere of influence over the executive government, but in practice the reforms did not bring administrative responsibility into the hands of the Indians. In 1917, eight years later, the British government declared its policy of associating Indians in every branch of the administration and the gradual development of self-government in India as an integral part of the British Empire. This declaration, however, once more stressed the idea of gradualism based upon successive installments. Moreover, the British authorities, as benevolent rulers, were to be the judges of the times and circumstances of the installments, and the Indians were to receive additional responsibility according as they showed willingness to coöperate. The major British provinces were to be the scenes for the experiment, where some authority would be granted to the Indians for observation and "control," in the expectation that these areas would be enlarged to include the whole provincial government.

Besides, an all-India central government was kept in view in which, too, authority would be gradually shifted from Brit-

The Renaissance of Asia

ish authorities to Indian, until India would be on a self-governing basis, like Canada or Australia. In 1919, as already mentioned, these declarations and promises were embodied in the Indian Act, the preamble of which stated that this progressive policy would be carried out as rapidly as possible, and also that within a ten-year period a commission would investigate the working of the 1919 legislation and advise to what extent additional installments of self-government might be granted. This commission, known as the Sir John Simon Commission, was appointed in November, 1927, and made its report in May, 1930. It recommended a complete federation of India so organized as to include the native princes, with the hope that a plan could be devised which the native princes would join voluntarily. To promote the idea of federation, three Indian round-table conferences were held, at the end of which the British government set forth proposals for a Federation of India. A government select committee of both houses of Parliament reported, in October, 1934, on this scheme of federation. With the white paper of March, 1933, also available for legislative information, the Act of 1935 was passed by Parliament after long and acrimonious discussion. It provided (1) for an all-Indian Federation, (2) for provincial autonomy, and (3) for responsible government with safeguards. The federal nature of the act, the special position of the Indian princes, the reservation of powers to the governors both in the provinces and in the central government, the problems of finance, transportation, defense, foreign affairs, railroads, and communications, national debt—all enter in to make this constitution unique in its stupendous and overwhelming intricacies. Today, experimentally in force in the provinces only, it is at this very moment that the setting up of the central machinery is receiving serious consideration.*

It is obvious from the stark statements just made that the new constitution is a bold and exceedingly complicated experiment in imperial policy, easily the most far-reaching ever attempted by the British.

The world-wide British Empire has been a constitutional experiment station for several hundred years, and, naturally, federal experiments in Canada, Australia, and the United States were drawn upon in the thirty years' effort to devise a constitution for India. Exact and specific information must be limited in this brief summary. There are most elaborate distinctions between federal and local powers, and with a federal court, to see that these distinctions are duly observed. Amendment is exceedingly difficult and has to be achieved through the British Parliament. In India the provinces were not self-governing, and therefore the constitution confers on them autonomy, which they did not possess before. The states of the native princes definitely surrender a considerable measure of their former authority in order to fit into the federal scheme. The combination of the princes with British India gives the federation another unique character and many peculiarities. The federal authority is uniform over the British

* Lord Linlithgow, Viceroy of India, "Give Federation the Trial It Deserves" (*Indian Information Series*, Vol. 4, No. 21, January 15, 1939), a speech delivered at the annual meeting of the Associated Chambers of Commerce of India on December 9, 1938. Additional constitutional information is available in Arthur Berriedale Keith, *A Constitutional History of India, 1600–1935*.

provinces, but need not be over the territories of the princes. Besides, federal legislative and executive authority may well vary among the native states because they are entering the federation voluntarily, at least in theory. Authority between the federation and its different units has been elaborately assigned to one or to the other, and provisions have been made that certain powers be exercised by both central and local governments. The governor general, for example, has the power of granting certain authority either to the federation or to its divisions in the field of legislation or finance for experimental purposes, even though this is not provided for in the constitution itself. The governors of the provinces are subject to the governor general, who in turn is, of course, under the secretary of state in London.

In Canada and Australia, with whose constitutions innumerable comparisons could be made, the federal governments are in possession of full responsibility; but this is not true in India, for defense and foreign relations are reserved for the governor general, subject to the home government. Amendment of the Australian and Canadian constitutions can be made only with the consent of their own provincial governments, their Parliaments, and also, in Australia, by means of popular referendum. A change in the Canadian constitution, owing to the peculiar circumstance that the French Canadians have a privileged position, has to have the additional approval of the British Parliament. In India amendment is wholly in the hands of the British Parliament. Judicial power in Canada rests ultimately with the privy council in Great Britain, whereas in Australia the jurisdiction of the privy council has not been called into service. In India, constitutional questions may well start on their way in various courts though the final decision rests in the privy council in London. In recent months hearty efforts have been made to establish responsible governments in the provinces in the hope that experience in provincial cabinets and provincial legislatures will prove that, when the federal government is reorganized under the constitution, the Indians will have proved their competence to play a significant part in the federation as well as in the local government. At least half the total population of the native states and at least half the state seats in the federal upper chamber must be represented before the constitution is put into operation.

Interesting indeed would it be to analyze this amazing constitutional scheme and to compare its features more fully with those of other and somewhat similar federal constitutions, ancient and modern, especially the sections relating to federal railways and transportation, defense, external affairs, ecclesiastical matters, the civil services now being taken over by men of color, finance, pensions, and the numerous other problems of a modern state.

The provisions for the central government are the most complicated of the whole machinery because the native rulers of Indian states have to delegate powers to the federal authority. The principles of self-government and responsibility are conceded, but defense, foreign affairs, and ecclesiastical matters are quite removed from the federal legislature and the federal executive and placed in the hands of the governor general alone. He also has special responsibility in five fields:

(1) Prevention of any grave threats to the peace and tranquillity of India or any part thereof. (2) Safeguarding of the financial standing and credit of the federation. (3) Protection of the rights of the Indian states and the legitimate interests of minorities and of the rights of legitimate interests of the public services. (4) Prevention of commercial discrimination. (5) Control of any matter which affects the administration of any department under the direction and control of the governor general.[10]

In brief, the governor general is expected to be guided mainly by the advice of his ministers, but in any crisis he may take over the whole administration of India. The intention, however, is that he should not exercise such powers except in the direst emergencies. Adverse critics of the federal proposals are divided between those who are convinced that the checks and restrictions are so strong that no real freedom and responsibility will accrue to the Indian ministers and, on the other hand, those who think that so much has been given to the Indians that the governor general will become a figurehead. In the provincial field the dualism of authority, or dyarchy, has been abolished and a unitary government under the governor appointed by the king has been established. The governor is advised by a council of ministers who are responsible to the elected legislature and who have full powers in the whole field of provincial administration. However, the governor has reserve powers which he may exercise in the event of a complete breakdown; but again it is intended that the Indians will actually rule the provinces. Drafted by skilled

---
[10] *The Economist, A Survey of India To-day,* p. 2, December 12, 1936.

British statesmen, prepared for during a period of thirty years and applicable to 350 million people, nearly one-fifth of the world's population, the proposed changes, in their revolutionary character, must be studied in the light of the vastness of the subcontinent that we call India, with a territory the size of the United States east of the Rockies and a population three times as large.

Even in the constitutional history of the British Empire, violence or the threat of violence have not been unknown phenomena. In Canada the rebellion of 1837, followed by Lord Durham's report, with the heated conflicts between French Canadian and English Canadian, was temporarily solved by the union of Ontario and Quebec in 1840, and again settled by a federal union of the whole of Canada in 1867. In South Africa, problems in the early 18th and 19th centuries involving Bantu, Boer, and Briton caused many constitutional crises, with questions of federation, union, sovereignty, suzerainty, leading ultimately to a union under the defeated Boers, now turned into British subjects. If these problems required each a century for solution by constitutional means, then India, with acute economic, political, and religious problems, quite inevitably challenges British statesmanship almost as heavily as present-day questions of European foreign policy. British constitutional history in the 18th and 19th centuries developed by slow-motion procedure, but India, plunged into power politics, modern industry, agricultural revolution, renaissance in the Moslem and in the Hindu world, overwhelmed by increase of population versus subsistence, and without vacant frontiers, impatiently awaits rapid solution of its pressing problems, including those of education, language, sanitation, budgets, and taxation.

The numerous specific provisions of the Act of 1935 need to be interpreted not only in their bearing upon the renaissance of Asia, but also as composing an instrument gradually transferring to the rising nationalism of India the control of its own economic life—in itself a startling revolution in the economic order of the whole British Empire. Self-government in Canada, Australia, New Zealand, and South Africa has given to these respective peoples control of their internal taxation, protective tariffs, immigration, foreign affairs, and even the right to declare war; and has also placed them in charge of internal improvements, patents and copyright, railroads, canals, hydroelectric power, broadcasting, and the like. In short, they are set up as practically independent among the nations of the world, but held together by common traditions, common memories, the advantages of creditor-debtor arrangements, mutual trade, and mutual defense.

Americans have been confused by Gandhi's fasts and other activities directed against the native rulers, and hence a further word of explanation may be welcome. His controversies have at times been with the Indian princes of the native states, who under British suzerainty rule about one-third of the territory and one-third of the population of India. Gandhi and the Indian Congress wish these princes to introduce a more democratic government, to reform their administrations, in short to catch up with British India in political and social policy. The British viceroy, it is true, can bring pressure on these princes; but he is naturally reluctant to do so. Gandhi's technique is so to stir up India, through the nation-wide Congress party, that the Indian-manned provincial governments in British India will threaten to resign and thereby create great confusion. To avoid these disruptions, the viceroy has recently intervened. Gandhi picked out a small native state, so that the viceroy's task was relatively easy, but nevertheless a precedent for intervention on the side of democracy is set. In fact, a short time ago the viceroy at the annual meeting of the Indian chamber of princes publicly admonished them to reform their governments, to avoid absenteeism, and to spend their revenues on their subjects rather than on themselves. Early in 1939, the Congress program was summed up in *The Manchester Guardian Weekly* (of March 17, 1939) as follows: Self-determination for India; complete confidence in Gandhi; opposition to British foreign policy as pro-Fascist; admiration for the courage and determination of the Arabs in Palestine; and anxiety regarding the position of Indians overseas, especially in the British Empire outside of India.[11]

Will India with her 222 languages, her many peoples as different from each other as the peoples of Europe, but with memories and traditions originally and fundamentally Asiatic, be able to unify her life under Hindu-Mohammedanism, her two greatest traditions, with sufficient attachment to the West to remain in the family of Western commonwealths? Will the Japanese advance be stopped at Singapore so that southern Asia will have a life separate and distinct from that of eastern Asia, where some fusion of Japanese and Chinese traditions will continue to occur?

---
[11] P. 207, March 17, 1939.

The most ardent British opponent of the Constitution of 1935 is quite willing to admit that India, thousands of miles away, cannot be held by force, but must be attached to the British world by consent and by her own decision. This Constitution of 1935 is a determined effort to give India dominion home rule as speedily as possible in the hope that she will be able to take over the conduct of her own affairs with sufficient good will toward the Western world to wish to remain on friendly terms with it.

As the day for putting the federal part of the constitution into operation approaches, crises and disquieting rumors will be common. The All-India Congress Party, dominated by the Hindus, and the All-India Moslem League will almost certainly be in constant political conflict. Already most of the provincial governments have fallen into Hindu hands, and in several of the provinces the Moslems are planning to use the Hindu weapon of civil disobedience to right their wrongs. A recent writer has said, "It is lamentably true that the Reforms, by arousing the ambitions of the Hindus and the anxieties of the Moslems, have given a new emphasis to Hindu-Moslem competition. The canon of tolerance set up by the British in pre-Reform days, when a neutral authority restricted Hindu-Moslem rivalry to narrow spheres, is rapidly being broken down."[12]

But on the other hand, over great areas, the new constitution, now two years in actual operation in the provinces, has met with success to a degree beyond expectation. The Congress ministers have received the sympathy and the coöpera-

---
[12] "Minorities in India," *The Times*, January 29, 1939.

tion of the British governors at every move, as well as the loyal aid of the Indian Civil Service. The viceroy's words of September 21, 1936, are still sound in 1939, "The British people and Parliament have seen fit to offer to India a constitution which by its liberal principles stands in such impressive contrast to those political tendencies which are evident over wide areas of the world."[13]

Americans, by heritage and tradition conscious of Europe, have not hitherto focused their attention sharply on what is going on in Asia. The evolution of constitutional government in India may well be, in the long view, more important than its perhaps temporary collapse in parts of Europe.[14] Thus no man knows his own times in its entirety, but, intent on the transformation of his own particular world, may be unaware of the emergence of a new world before his eyes.

---

[13] "His Excellency the Viceroy's Speech to Both the Houses of the Legislature in the Legislative Assembly Building on September 21, 1936," *International Conciliation*, p. 537, November, 1936.

[14] Now that another war has broken out, constitutional developments are being held in abeyance. But the status described in these pages, written early in 1939, is not materially changed. The pattern of demand and delay of the World War is, in general, repeating itself. Solution awaits the end of the war, for, although there have been several testings of strength, all parties seem agreed not to force an extreme crisis.

THE ROLE OF INDO-CHINA
IN ASIA

MELVIN M. KNIGHT

PROFESSOR OF ECONOMICS
IN THE UNIVERSITY OF CALIFORNIA

Lecture delivered April 10, 1939

THE ROLE OF INDO-CHINA IN ASIA

WHAT IS INDO-CHINA?—Indo-China consists of one colony and four protectorates of France, federated by an Indo-Chinese Union which the French set up in 1887. The present total area of 277,505 square miles (more than that of California and Nevada combined) dates from the fixing of the Siamese frontier in 1907. This area stretches a thousand miles from north to south on the tropical mainland of southeast Asia. Half the boundary is seacoast, the rest being shared by China, British Burma, and Siam. The total population of 23 millions is very unevenly distributed, four-fifths of it being on one-tenth of the surface.

This populous tenth consists of the coastal plain of the Red River in the north, that of the Mekong in the south, and the connecting coastal strip of Annam; hence the figure that Indo-China is "a pole balanced by two rice-baskets." The rest of the country is largely mountainous, interspersed with jungles which contain some settled clearings. Any unused land in the plains is quickly swallowed by jungle. Angkor is the famous example. This vast stone capital of the Khmers or Cambodians practically disappeared from the memory of man after its abandonment in the 15th century. There is no considerable space in Indo-China where the climate permits of permanent settlements of Europeans.

The oldest numerous people now inhabiting Indo-China is the Khmer or Cambodian. A thousand years ago this civilization and another of Hindu or Hindu-Malay origin, that of Champa, occupied two-thirds of the country, the Khmers in the southwest and the Chams in the southeast. In the far

FIG. I. FRENCH INDO-CHINA

northeast the Red River delta had been occupied for many centuries by a third invading group, the Annamites. This non-Chinese people from the Tibetan-Chinese borderland had fallen under the domination and tutelage of the Chinese, but were just getting freedom in all but name—in 931 A.D. The Annamites did not take the southward road to empire for another five hundred years, after they had again been briefly subjected to China (1414-1428) and again had broken loose. Some authorities believe that there were Thai groups in this area as early as the fourth century A.D. These people have also come from the Tibetan-Chinese borderland, passing into upper Tonking, Laos, and Siam. They did not play a major part in the Indo-Chinese drama until they came into conflict with the Khmers about the 12th century.

When the French began their serious conquest in 1858, Champa had long disappeared before the Annamite southward advance. Annam had also taken Cochin-China, first the eastern part when Champa was annihilated, then the remainder from Cambodia. One Thai infiltration had followed the Mekong River southward through Laos, leaving many isolated communities of earlier inhabitants. The other had followed the Mena River southwestward and made itself master of Siam. By 1858, when the French took Saigon, Cambodia was crumbling between the Siamese and Annamite millstones. The petty principalities and independent communities of Laos were similarly ripe for absorption. Here Siam was in a position to take the largest share, Annam most of the remainder. Some might have gone to Burma, and some even to China, but for the intervention of France.

Formation of French Indo-China.—France took Cochin-China in two gulps. The eastern half was relinquished by Annam in a treaty of 1862 which made the western half easy to take in 1867. In the same treaty, the emperor of Annam gave up any rights he might have over Cambodia, paving the way to a French protectorate set up in 1863. This protectorate isolated western Cochin-China from Annam and gave the French access to Laos, most of which was glad to be protected by anybody from the Siamese, Annamites, and Chinese.

Siam did not readily abandon her claims to Cambodia and Laos, which were at least as strong as those relinquished by Annam. The French were never in a position to force a settlement until after their *entente cordiale* with Great Britain in 1904. Then it became too dangerous for Siam to count on the deterring effect of British interests. The present boundary, as fixed in 1907, is very favorable to Indo-China.

Difficulties with Siam, and the discovery that the Mekong did not afford access to South China, early led the French to shift their main activities to Tonking. Blocked there in navigation and trading schemes which they asserted were covered by their treaty with Annam, they seized the cities and forts of the Red River delta in 1873. Unable to meet this crisis alone, the emperor of Annam appealed to China for aid. In order to get it he acknowledged a Chinese sovereignty which had been inoperative and practically forgotten for centuries. Armed bands from South China made the French a vast amount of trouble for a decade. The French might well have been ejected had they not brought naval pressure to bear upon the Chinese Empire elsewhere. Finally, in 1884–85, China abandoned all claims to Annam and its subject territory, Tonking. France was now in a position to "pacify" Tonking and to reduce Annam itself to a protectorate.

"Divide and rule."—French colonial policy under the Third

Knight: Indo-China

Republic was turning away from direct rule to "association," the central idea of which is to preserve native civilizations as far as possible and make them run themselves under French supervision. "Respect for native institutions" is convenient in many ways. Thus it justified the continuance of forced labor, corporal punishment, trial methods which had been abolished in France in the 18th century, and so on, provided they were used only on natives and by natives in authority. There is little now of what is technically known as "forced labor." Occasionally the French conscience has been stirred by beatings of natives by European foremen on isolated plantations, but as a rule these things have not become generally known. It may be noted by way of comparison that in the Philippines the Americans created a system of laws for natives which could be imposed by and upon Americans.

The "association" of peoples, with "respect for native institutions," also has a variety of meanings to fit special plans and circumstances. The Annamites formed a two-thirds majority in all Indo-China, all the way from Tonking through Annam to the western part of Cochin-China. Memories of their imperial position were too fresh for the comfort of the French conquerors. Therefore it seemed advisable to respect and foster local differences. It was not very hard to extinguish what remained of the prestige of the Annamite imperial throne in Tonking. There also, the Annamite mandarinate or bureaucracy was systematically undermined and in part replaced by a native elite dependent upon the French administration. This decapitated Tonkinese unit is sometimes called a protectorate, though it certainly is not a protected state, and though it bears considerable resemblance to the outright colony of Cochin-China.

In Annam, on the contrary, the prestige of the throne and mandarinate was assiduously built up. This populous and relatively poor country remained backward and inexpensive to rule, while the French applied their main energies to richer Tonking and Cochin-China. The backwardness which was so enthusiastically respected helped to widen the differences between the Annamites of Annam and the increasingly "evolved" or Europeanized Annamites in the other two Annamite countries. Tonking was completely separated from Annam in 1897, after suitable preparation.

The Indo-Chinese Union had been set up ten years earlier to coördinate the French administrations of the units as they should ripen and take their places in it. Laos could be added when Siam's claims were taken care of and Annam's fully extinguished. With a license equal to the poetic, Laos is called a protectorate. It is really eight districts, some with native rulers and some without—a unit only with respect to its French administration. In some particulars, which need not be discussed here, the Kwangchowwan territory, leased from China since 1898, is under the general government of the Indo-Chinese Union, and is sometimes inaccurately referred to as a sixth member.

Economic development.—Before the French came, Indo-China was a loosely articulated series of communities, producing in the main for their own consumption. Locally, there were families run by patriarchs, villages run by notables among these heads of families, and larger districts more or

Knight: Indo-China 43

less coördinated by notables among the notable. Contracts between such local units and political or economic centers struck the French newcomers as more like treaty relationships than an integrated system.

To justify itself and pay its way, a French system of control had to create exports in order to import technical equipment, organizing skill, and consumption goods to give European personnel a European standard of living. Local surpluses of produce must not only be made to appear, but they must also be moved to the sea by an appropriate transport system. Even the maintenance of order and the protection of frontiers according to French ideas called for reliable inland communications.

The first railroad, from Hanoi to the Chinese frontier near Lungchow, was useful mainly for defense and internal "pacification" in upper Tonking. It was very expensive to build and never paid. Lately it has been in the news because of a motor road on to Nanning on the West River and an extension of the railway itself to that point, which is presumably nearing completion. Another narrow-gauge line connects the Gulf of Tonking with Yunnanfu in South China, across hundreds of miles of jagged mountains and jungle. Built after the Boxer Rebellion of 1900, following an insufficient survey and accompanied by notorious graft and shocking mortality, this scenic line has never paid, either. Now that the two railways just mentioned might recoup some of their losses by carrying munitions to China, the Japanese are advising the French to refrain. This advice seems likely to be taken, since Japan holds the island of Hainan, which partly closes the Gulf of Tonking and makes Kwangchowwan untenable in case of real trouble. Let no one suppose that France could muster in Indo-China any large fraction of the naval and air force which Japan could apply suddenly at any time. The British are less vulnerable. They can better afford to gamble against an outcome of the "China incident" which would make Hongkong and other coastal possessions of dubious value anyhow. Southwest China seems likeliest to get supplies over the new motor road from the Burmese railhead at Lashio to Yunnanfu.

Engineering difficulties in parts of Annam where the mountains come down to the sea postponed until 1936 the completion of the Haiphong–Saigon line. There are some branches, including one into central Laos which is supposed to join the Siamese network eventually. The original plan also calls for joining old fragments to make a through railway from Saigon into Cambodia and on to the Siamese frontier at Aranya, west of Angkor, from whence there is already a line to Bangkok. Delays in carrying out the old plans have been in large part justified by the construction of some 22,000 miles of primary and secondary motor roads. These highly publicized highways are adequate (as are those of the Dutch East Indies), but the best constructed roads in this corner of Asia are in the Philippines.

Land communications between Indo-China and Siam have been greatly stimulated by a commercial treaty of 1937, following quickly upon the Japanese invasion of China. The Siamese had long been inclined to wink at the smuggling of Japanese goods into Cambodia and Laos along a frontier too long, wild, and thinly peopled for adequate watching. With these goods, and often enough without them, came opium. Smoking places were running openly in Indo-China in 1934, and one might doubt the passionate desire of French authorities to suppress the traffic entirely, but at least they did not like to see the tremendous taxes imposed upon it undermined by bootlegging. Faced by the far more active menace of Japan, the Siamese suddenly decided to coöperate with the French.

Of all the public works created under French administration in Indo-China, those directed toward water control are the least subject to criticism. Some of these keep the treacherous Red River from flooding lower Tonking. The problem of the more sluggish Mekong in Cochin-China has been one of drainage. Here enough dirt has been dredged from the channels in a half-century to fill the Suez Canal, and two thousand miles of major and minor canals have been dug, besides. Nearly five million acres of land have been opened to cultivation at a cost of about three dollars per acre. If anything which may be called an economic miracle has been performed in Indo-China, it has rested upon this cheap land and upon native labor at less than twenty-five cents a day.

The great bulk of the export purchasing power which has financed the remaking of Indo-China has come from rice, a native crop raised much as it has been raised for centuries. Plantation methods were tried after the World War on newly drained land where big fields were available. Some of the equipment was clever, but the ventures failed. Hand labor was too cheap relative to technical direction and machinery, except when unusual demand and high prices for rice prevailed, temporarily providing a market which could not be supplied with the hand labor available.

Cochin-China raised practically all the export rice, Tonking sometimes failing to feed itself. The Cochin-Chinese rice-growing area increased twelvefold in sixty years, reaching a peak about 1930, while the population rose only from one to a little over four millions. Exports rose meanwhile from a few tons annually to a million and a half. The revenue to which this gave rise did not go to enrich the growers. It has often been said that the whole Indo-Chinese economy, with its vast imports of machinery and other materials, supporting a French investment of two-thirds of a billion dollars, has rested on the backs of the native rice farmers in Cochin-China. Even beyond 1930, after all the stimulation to coal mining and plantation crops such as rubber, the value of exported rice still exceeded that of all other exports combined. From the start, another native product, dried fish, has never fallen very far short of second place.

France has taken the glory and left to little Cochin-China most of the burden of playing mother country to the Indo-Chinese Union. In 1934, Paul Bernard put the taxes collected in Cochin-China at 35 per cent of the income of each inhabitant. The nearest competitor in Indo-China was Cambodia, with 18 per cent. Taxes in France were estimated at around 25 per cent, but French incomes were large enough to support far higher deductions than those of a hot country where a peasant proprietor is barely able to keep his family alive by the hardest kind of hand work, and a hired laborer gets less today than twenty-five of our cents per day. And Indo-China under French rule has become an expensive country. Above the marginal type of livelihood on which a native family could continue to exist, prices were as high on an average, and many of them were much higher, in 1934 than those of France. And living costs were so high in France at that time that American official personnel received a bonus in the form of a special exchange rate in order to maintain respectability.

"Cochin-China," said a native delegate to the French Superior Council of the Colonies, "pays annually to the general budget more than forty million piasters [then roughly $24,000,000, at 10 francs per piaster]. The sums thus taken from our revenues have been expended in Tonking, in Annam and in Laos, so one may say that it is we who have paid for the Tonkinese dykes, the Mandarin Road and the Laotian penetration routes." He added the cliché that Cochin-China had played the honorable but onerous role of mother country, one which France should have assumed, "with the honor and the responsibility."

Problems of maturity: economic.—The Indo-Chinese economic problem, like that of many other imperial possessions, has developed aspects since 1929 which were latent but little considered earlier. In the years before the World War, Indo-China was exporting more than she imported, in most years by a good many millions of our dollars. Yet France was taking only a little more than half enough of these exports to pay for the goods she sent to Indo-China. She got paid indirectly for Saigon export rice, the great bulk of which was sold in the Far East, particularly to China. This mediocre product also helped to eke out the Philippine supply, so that the Islands could produce sugar, copra, tobacco, and Manila hemp for the high-priced American market. British Malaya imported rice in order to specialize in the growing of rubber for export. Java bought low-grade Cochin-Chinese rice in order to export her own superior grades at higher prices. Japan imported it from time to time up to the Indo-Chinese tariff of 1928, particularly hostile to the Japanese goods which might otherwise have been used to pay for the rice.

Then the twilight of 1929 descended upon this paradise of multilateral trade and payments. One country after another entered a wild competition to see which could cut out the most imports. Every import is an export for somebody, and his means of payment for somebody else's exports. Carried to its logical conclusion, such a world-wide policy would reduce each country to autarchy or self-containment, supplemented by barter between pairs of countries, each receiving just the value of what it furnished. From the purely economic point of view, trade between distant parts of an empire is no different from "foreign" trade, or that across political frontiers. Whether it pays to carry Indo-Chinese rice all the way to France, and French cotton goods all the way back, turns out to be in large part a question of what the French call the "cost of distance."

If France took more than a quarter of Indo-China's rice exports, she got more than her people wanted for food. The main use which could be and was made of more than this was to mix it into stock feed, replacing corn imported from Argentina and elsewhere. Rice is a mediocre feed, regardless of the cost of hauling so bulky a product over so vast a distance. Moreover, Argentina and the other corn exporters cut down their purchases of French goods as France shut out their means of payment. The encouragement of corn at the expense of rice in Indo-China had some effect, but most rice land does not lend itself to the shift, which often is uneconomical where it is nevertheless possible.

Rubber, tea, and other products which France did want were encouraged in Indo-China by special aid to planters, financed in the long run by sales at high prices which were imposed upon French consumers by high tariffs and quotas, or by direct bonuses taken out of the duties on French imports from politically "foreign" sources. This method of taxing consumers in the mother country for the support of enterprise overseas by means of higher prices is one of the most insidious ever devised. The two excuses for it are, first, that the colony must be aided to avoid financial collapse and social chaos, and second, that the imports pay for exports. An "assimilated" Indo-Chinese tariff favors French goods in return for a tariff in the mother country which favors Indo-Chinese goods. So the import of unwanted rice into France, at prices which must include an immense "cost of distance," is balanced by imports into Indo-China of goods from the high-priced French market for the millions of poor native consumers. The quantity of French goods which these tiny incomes can buy depends upon the prices, which are extremely high as compared with those for which Japan, or even the United States, would lay down similar articles in Indo-China.

Even where there is a difference in quality, the misfit between French goods and Annamite incomes is often striking.

The superiority of cheap French shoes at a dollar over Japanese ones which might be had for twenty cents is little comfort to the workman who has only twenty cents. An attempt of the Dutch East Indies to approach a balance of exports and imports in the trade with Japan broke down in 1934 over this problem. The Japanese knew very well, and so did the Dutch, that a social upheaval would result if the native population were forced to pay the minimum prices for which Dutch goods could be sold. Our Trade Commissioner in Batavia told me of a bet made in a club, and won, that a man could be outfitted completely, from head to toe, in European-style clothes for the equivalent of two dollars. The items bought were of Japanese manufacture. At that time the cheapest white cotton suit cost more than that in Saigon, without the hat, shirt, tie, belt, shoes, socks, garters, and handkerchief which the winner of the wager had to supply.

As the depression and its accompanying trade restrictions continued, Japan cut out Saigon rice, and even China decreased her consumption materially. Faced with the lower prices of exports and the curtailment of the American market, the Philippines planted the additional rice they needed. Java, with her rubber and sugar trade depressed and her own high-grade rice a drug in the world market, cut down her imports. Even British Malaya began planting more rice to keep from having to buy it with rubber, which the French were more and more replacing from their Indo-Chinese plantations.

In the 'twenties, France had been taking barely more than a fifth of Indo-China's total exports. By 1934 she was taking more than half, and in 1936 she took more than 60 per cent.

In that year, 58 per cent of Indo-China's export rice went to France, as compared with a share which rarely rose to a fourth before the depression. Instead of selling Indo-China twice what she bought in return, France now owed the Union annual commodity balances. They were not remitted in cash, of course, but went a small fraction of the way toward meeting the claims of investors upon Indo-China.

Such figures merely illustrate the important point that, under present conditions, Indo-China is an economic burden to the mother country. The roughly balanced trade is as truly barter in its effects as though it were carried on between distant and independent states, but has special disadvantages. It is artificialized by trying to protect a large French investment, and responsibilities of a political, social, and military nature go with it. Its organization hinders more economical relationships between each party and its nearer neighbors. The fallacy behind such arrangements was well expressed by a deputy in the French Chamber back in 1931. He remarked that Frenchmen seemed to suffer from the delusion that anything obtained from a colony was free.

Nor can Indo-China be counted upon as an asset in the event of war. To be that, it would have to provide more power of some sort than the amount required to defend it. What zinc, tin, rubber, tropical wood for gunstocks, and other war materials Indo-China could supply to France in an emergency must be transported along a route that would hardly be worth defending from the likely combinations of enemies in any serious war. Japan might have difficulty in taking Indo-China, especially without having really pacified South China first, but she would have little trouble in making the country valueless to France. As to the heavier types of Indo-Chinese produce such as rice, corn, coal, and dried fish, the problem of their disposal in wartime would involve painful readjustments.

Problems of maturity: social and political.—First, there are too many Frenchmen in Indo-China—almost as many on the public payrolls as there are British in India, which has fifteen times the native population. As the localism of the society has been undermined by central organization, native notables are no longer satisfied and coöperative in local positions which have lost their importance. Hence there must be dissatisfaction at the top of the French-formed native elite until the highest offices are open to it, whereupon the French will be swamped. Moreover, to find the number and quality of native subordinates needed, at least three times as many have to be trained or partly trained to select from. The two-thirds or more who receive no jobs or poor ones form an element which is far more dangerous than the same number would be if left untrained.

At the bottom, French petty clerks, doorkeepers, and the like hold positions which natives could fill just as well, and live in a style poor enough to detract from French prestige but good enough to excite native jealousy. The supposed rigors of the civil service examinations have been so generally evaded in the past that the service is stuffed with incompetents who do not know the languages or the country. Rules against proprietorship and business enterprise on the part of public employees were pretty openly circumvented a decade ago by such devices as importing brothers-in-law and fathers-in-law for figureheads. This condition may have improved in Cochin-China, where it was notorious—I did not think to inquire when I was there very briefly, five years ago. Some Frenchmen of quite incredibly unsuitable types have held such positions as customs officers at remote points, poisoning French prestige in all the five or six ways one thinks of first.

One object of the tariff of 1928 and the legislation following it was the undermining of the Chinese community, particularly in Cochin-China. At the top were merchants and millers in control of the rice trade. Below these were tradesmen, artisans, skilled clerical assistants, and other elements of real value to the country. The tariff on Chinese products was followed by head taxes, business taxes, and other measures so severe that a large fraction of the Chinese left the country. Cholon, the milling and commercial town alongside Saigon, was reduced in six years from the busiest urban community in Cochin-China to a dead and half-empty shell. Though I saw none of the grass which Europeans assured me grew in the streets, the general appearance of the place lent itself to the figure. The mistake was in large measure corrected after 1934.

The decline of the Hindu usurers (chettys) was less to be regretted. After widely scattered and serious Annamite disturbances in 1930, a system of agricultural credit for small borrowers, under public supervision, was gradually spread over the country. Though a serious effort has been made to get interest charges down at least to 12 per cent, most of the lending is still done by the usurers, at rates often twice as high as that.

Alexandre Varenne, Socialist vice-president of the Chamber of Deputies, who served as governor general of Indo-China from 1925 to 1927, opened many public employments and skilled professions to natives, removing the absurd rule that such people must take French citizenship. It helped to reduce the percentage of French employees at the level of doorkeeper, and did some good higher up, but it did not satisfy the superior and well-trained Annamites who wanted to be something in the country of their ancestors. The French community was seething with anger, and got Varenne recalled, but the Annamites were almost as dissatisfied with him on the opposite ground that he had not gone half far enough.

By 1934 there was a staggering list of businesses which "foreigners" (not including Frenchmen) were forbidden to conduct. It even included steamship agencies. Foreign banks and insurance companies were ordered to raise the percentage of French or Indo-Chinese employees to a degree which would have ruined them if they had strictly complied, as competent personnel in these categories was not available. Immense fines were imposed upon foreigners for infractions of rules which might well occur accidentally. Clients of foreign insurance companies so uniformly won large awards that some lines were abandoned, such as automobile coverage. This left the business to French firms, who incurred either similar losses or the hatred of native claimants who had learned bad habits with the connivance of the authorities and now began to regard Frenchmen as merely the least desirable class of foreigners.

The list of native and foreign grievances which I collected would read like a scandal sheet, and I really do not mean this for an attack upon French colonial policy, which is above the average in many respects. Like the Annamites, we may be tempted to make comparisons with the American treatment of the Philippines, remembering, however, that the Americans have been inclined to be soft about taking care of their own interests in colonial matters. For one thing, the fact that they generally get out eventually appeals to the Annamite imagination. Nor is one law for whites and nonwhites an evidence of good faith to be sneezed at.

One reason why more has been done about public works and social Europeanization in the Philippines than in Indo-China, and in less than half the time, is to be found in trade policy. For decades we let the Philippines sell dear in our market and use the proceeds largely to buy cheap in others. The commodity balance ran heavily against the mother country during long years when that between France and Indo-China was doing the opposite. Our "assimilated" relationship with the Philippine tariff was notoriously in that region's favor, while, as Paul Bernard attempts to prove in detail, France's Indo-Chinese tariff system worked heavily to the colony's disadvantage. We certainly upset the French, Dutch, and British in the Far East by offering the Philippines independence when they could detach themselves to any reasonable degree from a partnership which gave them most of the benefits and us most of the burdens.

So much has been said of the "white man's burden" that it is rather a comfort to find it becoming more and more an actual condition. It is very likely that when all the bad debts and sour investments have been written off we shall discover that we have really done a good deal for backward peoples, and at considerable expense to ourselves. As to gratitude on their part, that should never be expected by the givers of good gifts. Even a few Frenchmen are now beginning to believe that much of France's economic nightmare comes from uneconomical dealings with her own far corners of the earth.

The profits which come from land because it is newly developed, and from labor because it is freshly exposed to a different standard of living and inexperienced with a real wage system, are impermanent. Land gets recapitalized in terms of its earnings, and native workers sometimes raise their sights even faster than they do their productivity. "Natives," like other people, get used to levels of consumption, and cannot be blamed for wanting what they can see others enjoy. Public order is a priceless boon where it has been absent, but it soon comes to be taken for granted. Condescending familiarity toward "natives" is certainly preferable to brutality, but it does not forever take the place of genuine respect. Unfortunately, these things sound less indulgent in English than they do when Frenchmen say them repeatedly about each other.

The future of Indo-China.—A living human burden cannot always be dumped when it begins to feel heavy. Should France give Indo-China to Japan, to Germany, or to Italy? Should she reconstitute the Annamite Empire and give it independence, or free the parts of the Union separately and leave them to face a greedy world as best they can? Would it be feasible and proper to attempt a Philippine type of solution, such as many Annamites clamor for, with gradual separation accompanied by aid and protection? Or can the problem of maturity be met within the French imperial system?

Much depends upon the outcome of the present strife in China. If the Far East is to have two strong powers, life will be much safer and more tolerable for smaller peoples than if there should be only one. If economic readjustment were the only question to be considered, the Indo-Chinese problem would be far simpler than that of the Philippines. It is easier to put an end to even mild exploitation than it is to excessive coddling. The populated areas of Indo-China are badly strung out and vulnerable, but the same is true of the Philippines. About 70 per cent of the Indo-Chinese population talks Annamite, which is a mixture of old dialects with acquisitions from the Chinese, Portuguese, Malay, French, and other languages. It was written in Chinese characters for centuries, and still is, though most native newspapers are now printed in the Latin alphabet—the *quoc ngu,* an adaptation originally made by Portuguese missionaries. A surprisingly small number of Indo-Chinese natives talk French even passably.

Most Frenchmen who think about Indo-China at all intend to keep it within the imperial system on some basis or other. That is probably the main answer, unless another should be imposed by the sheer force of events. The last thing France is likely to do, except from necessity, is to give the country to some totalitarian power. There seems to be at least that much sincerity in the *mission civilisatrice.*

The Renaissance of Asia

After a talk I gave at a German university last autumn, I was asked why countries which found colonies burdensome did not turn some over to Germany. It seemed to me that a significant item in the answer must consist of the fact that the burdens may be associated with a certain sense of obligation and of decency on the part of the "tutor" nations. My questioner's tone was that of a person who has triumphantly caught another in an inconsistency, so I tried to convey my idea in a counterquestion, Does the treatment by Germans of non-Germans in late years give suitable assurance that Germany can be trusted to fulfill obligations to subject peoples?

Perhaps the suggestion gives British, French, Dutch, and Belgian motives too much credit. Even if the improved behavior of such imperial nations is due in part to their defensive position, the fact of the behavior remains. Some people assure us that no profit can be made out of Manchuria, Ethiopia, China, Czechoslovakia, or Albania by stark and brutal domination. This view may be correct, but one may be allowed some misgivings. Perhaps we have been giving the human race at large too much credit for loving freedom and making trouble for oppressors. In short, who knows what devices for imposing serfdom, and what capacities for accepting it, these new types of states may dig up?

The tenth of Indo-China which contains most of the population should always be remembered as tropical, and seen against its background of mountains and jungles. These millions who swarm along the hot edges, fighting back trees with weaker tools than we have for slicing off weeds, do not have our confidence in ballot boxes or in the possibilities for a well-fed life. Certainly the individual feels his own life less precarious, now that the tigers and panthers have retreated behind the absolute fringe of the jungle and the Pasteur Institute has waged its war against disease germs and snake bites. While the jungle is actually receding, its menace to a whole society may slip out of mind until there is some little relaxation of vigilance. Yet the menace is always there, wrapped around mighty ruins, such as Angkor, of what man thought was permanent.

NOTE ON SOURCES: Paul Bernard, *Le Problème Economique Indochinois* (Paris, 1934) is the best general treatise on that subject. It is conveniently supplemented by the *Quarterly Review of Economic Conditions in Southeastern Asia*, issued by the United States Bureau of Foreign and Domestic Commerce, and by the fortnightly *Far Eastern Survey* of the Institute of Pacific Relations. J. Suignard, *Les Services Civiles de l'Indochine* (Paris, 1931) is particularly intimate and revealing. The report of the International Labour Office entitled *Labour Conditions in Indo-China* (Geneva, 1938) is excellent and largely firsthand. For a well-selected list of works, see the bibliography of Virginia Thompson, *French Indo-China* (New York, 1937), a workmanlike general treatise with the special merits of being recent and in English.

DOMESTIC FACTORS IN JAPANESE
FOREIGN POLICY

KAZUO KAWAI
INSTRUCTOR IN HISTORY
IN THE UNIVERSITY OF CALIFORNIA

Lecture delivered April 17, 1939

DOMESTIC FACTORS IN JAPANESE FOREIGN POLICY

IN ANY study of the renaissance of Asia, Japan demands attention as the first nation of that part of the world to challenge the traditional supremacy of the West. Especially within the last few years, since Japan has apparently set out to establish her hegemony over the entire Far East, Europe and America have come to regard with increasing irritation and apprehension this upstart who has learned the methods of Western imperialism all too well. The older established great powers are loud in their condemnation of this disconcerting youngster who reminds them too embarrassingly of their own turbulent adolescence which they would now like to forget, but if the world is to meet intelligently the problems caused by the rise of this newest of the imperialistic powers, it is necessary to go beyond mere denunciation and to study the reasons why Japan is acting as she is.

If it is permissible to use a very homely illustration, Japan may be likened to a youngster who persists in fighting his playmates. Merely restraining or punishing the boy will not permanently solve the difficulty. It is necessary to learn what forces impel him to be so pugnacious, so that the influences which predispose him to pugnacity may be corrected. The problem calls not for the services of a policeman, but for the services of the social case worker who would investigate the family background of the boy, the physician who would search for physical abnormalities, and the psychiatrist who would try to find out what mental twists and complexes caused this youngster to become so antisocial. Such investigation might reveal that the treatment does not call for punishments and disciplinary measures, that social ostracism or spanking might only aggravate the trouble, and that the proper corrective measures might consist of the opening up of wider horizons by sympathetic experts who would try to win the confidence of the suspicious and uncoöperative patient. It might even be revealed that the patient was merely unfortunate in the type of playmates whom he found in his neighborhood.

Japan today has the reputation of being an international troublemaker. A thorough investigation might reveal, however, that she is the victim of circumstances, a pawn of forces beyond her control, rather than a conscious molder of her own destiny. Her behavior in her international dealings may not be so much the product of a premeditated design as of a few serious physical and emotional ailments which force her into action over which she can exercise little volition. The problem of Japan unfortunately has been confused by the raising of moral issues with attendant emotionalism, when the problem is essentially a pathological one amenable to scientific treatment.

Any explanation of the foreign policy of Japan, therefore, necessitates the diagnosing of Japan's internal ills which influence her conduct. Many such ills have been attributed to her. To mention a few, there is the much publicized and obvious pressure of population.[1] There is also the fairly general

---
[1] Cf. Albert E. Hindmarsh, *The Basis of Japanese Foreign Policy* (Cambridge, 1936).

belief that Japan is suffering from a Messianic complex, that her rulers have delusions of grandeur and believe it to be their destiny to confer the benefits of their rule upon a foolishly resisting world.[2] Some hold that Japan's foreign policy is evidence that her leaders are intoxicated by the lust for power; others, that her foreign policy is dictated by fear, that the Japanese have been rendered frantic to the point of hysteria by the specters of a developing Russia and a reawakening China.[3] There is also the likelihood that Japan's conduct is the result of a terrific inferiority complex induced by her experiences of the past eighty years when she, as the lone nonwhite nation attempting to break into the society of great powers in a world which was apparently a white man's world, met with snubs and rebuffs, or, what was more galling, overextravagant compliments which smacked of a patronizing air. Her present blustering and bellicose attitude may therefore be the outburst of a long repressed resentment, or else may be mere compensation for an unadmitted lack of self-confidence.[4] Yet others hold that Japan's ills are not of so grave a character, that her present temper is but a normal temporary phase

[2] Robert T. Pollard, "Dynamics of Japanese Imperialism," *Pacific Historical Review*, Vol. 8, No. 1 (March, 1939), pp. 5–35, particularly pp. 16–27. Upton Close (pseudonym for Joseph Washington Hall), *Challenge Behind the Face of Japan* (New York, 1934), is a more extended but uncritical and sensationalized treatment of the same subject.

[3] Cf. G. E. Hubbard's criticism of Hindmarsh, *op. cit.*, for minimizing the "fear" complex; in *Pacific Affairs*, Vol. 9, No. 3 (September, 1936), pp. 474–475.

[4] Cf. the present writer's treatment of this inferiority complex in the attitude of Japanese industrialists and businessmen, in "Significance of Japanese Industrial and Commercial Growth," *Annals of the American Academy of Political and Social Science*, Vol. 193 (September, 1937), p. 135.

through which all adolescent nations just beginning to feel their power must inevitably pass.[5]

As intriguing as these suggested maladies are, no one of them seems to offer a fully adequate explanation for Japan's conduct, and the truth may well be that several of them, together with irritations from without, combine to drive Japan to her present feverish condition. Lack of space prevents an examination of all these possible afflictions, and hence it will be impossible to make a complete diagnosis, to say nothing of proposing the remedy. It is possible, however, to point out that one of the significant symptoms of the ailments troubling Japan is the struggle for political power raging within the country. An examination of this struggle might well shed light upon some of the domestic factors which influence Japanese foreign policy.

The fact that there is raging in Japan a most intense internal political strife may come as a surprise to some. With an emperor supposedly descended from the gods, wielding complete authority over fanatically loyal subjects who worship him as a deity, Japan would seem to be a country singularly free from the possibility of any internal strife. With willing submission to absolute authority, a docile but solidly united nation would seem to stand ready at hand to serve as a pliant instrument for the execution of whatever program the emperor and his intimates might arbitrarily decree. Such is the conception of Japan widely prevalent in America, a conception which even the Japanese themselves have at times con-

---

[5] Samuel van Valkenberg, *Elements of Political Geography* (New York, 1939), chs. i and xxvi.

sciously cultivated in an attempt to impress others, or to reassure themselves of their solidarity and strength.

Yet even the casual observer must have noted within recent years that assassinations and attempted *coups d'état* indicate that all is not harmonious even in this theocratic state. Surprised by evidences of strife in a nation in which they had expected to find no strife, some observers have jumped to the conclusion that Japan is hopelessly divided. They say that the present political strife is a sign that the archaic political, social, and particularly the economic structures of the country have become hopelessly shaky, that the existing order cannot withstand much more strain, and that therefore an economic boycott, a short major war, or a prolonged guerrilla warfare would suffice to bring about a collapse of the present regime. Her vaunted solidarity is no more, her feet are of clay, is the burden of several recent books written about Japan.[6]

The truth, of course, is that neither of these conceptions is correct. The picture of a solidly united Japan marching at the command of the all-highest emperor is but the nightmare of the alarmist or the fancy of the naïvely exultant patriot; while the opposing picture of an overstrained Japan seething with dissension and resorting to a last frantic military adventure in a vain attempt to ward off the collapse also is but a product of wishful thinking on the part of her enemies.

As a matter of fact, there has always been political strife throughout the history of Japan, for the character of the emperorship makes such political struggles inevitable. The

[6] The classic expression of this point of view is to be found in Freda Utley, *Japan's Feet of Clay* (London, 1936).

emperor has always been a figurehead, and although in theory he, as the Son of Heaven, is the source of all authority, that authority has always been exercised by some power behind the throne. The fundamental theory of the emperorship prevents him from exercising any active political power, for his function is to serve as the embodiment of the nation as a whole. He can perform this function of being the symbol of the entire nation only by remaining above politics. The instant he takes part in politics he must necessarily take sides on controversial issues, which means that he no longer represents the entire nation but only a single faction. To be emperor, he must remain politically neutral. He is a sort of a living flag, to be saluted by all, and waved around by every competing faction.

This means that the emperor must remain perfectly passive while the competition among the rival factions is fought out below him. Only after a particular faction has emerged decisively triumphant over all the others and has made its point of view prevail over the entire nation can the emperor throw the cloak of sanction over that position.[7] In other words, the position of the dominant group becomes the position of the nation, and thus the dominant group is the power behind the throne, although as soon as it loses power it may be repudiated by its successor as false advisers who have betrayed the best interest of the emperor.

[7] Yukio Ozaki, *Voice of Japanese Democracy* (Tokyo, 1918), p. 11, states, apropos of this point: "The sovereign has no mind of his own; the mind of the people is his mind, and on this principle our successive Emperors have acted. It implies the guiding of, as well as acting upon, the sentiments of the people."

Kawai: Japan 69

Inasmuch as there is no provision for the determination by constitutional means of who this power behind the throne shall be, it is inevitable that a struggle for the position should constantly go on. In very early times a council of patriarchal chieftains constituted the power behind the throne. In the 8th century, riding on a wave of popular religious fanaticism, the Buddhist priesthood came to control the throne. In the 10th century a family of court nobles, the Fujiwara family, through manipulation of imperial marriages, ruled as strong-willed fathers-in-law of weakling emperors. From the 13th to the 17th century, feudal lords fought constantly for the control of the puppet emperors. In 1603 the Tokugawa family, assuming the title of Shogun, or military dictator, became the power behind the throne and so remained until 1868.

Since the establishment in the 19th century of a modern constitutional government, this same struggle has persisted. The actual administration is carried on by a cabinet organized like the cabinets of all modern governments, but the struggle is over the question of the responsibility of the cabinet. The emperor, to be sure, supposedly appoints the cabinet, but the question still is, Who shall control the emperor when he appoints the cabinet? The power behind the throne is still the prize for the perennial political free-for-all in Japan.[8] In the past this struggle concerned no one but the Japanese, but

[8] The advice of the Genro, or Elder Statesmen, an extraconstitutional body, has invariably been followed since 1892 in the selection of the prime minister; but inasmuch as the Genro recommended the leader or the representative of the dominant element, the struggle for dominance continued perpetually. In essence, therefore, the element dominant at the moment is the power behind the throne. The extinction of the Genro with the recent death of the last member of this body can have no effect on this fundamental condition.

within recent years it has become significant to the rest of the world because it has come to have a bearing upon Japan's foreign policy.

Down to the time of the World War there were only two serious contenders for the position of the power behind the throne, namely, the bureaucracy and the political parties. As yet, the bureaucracy included both the military and the civilian officials, for, despite minor rivalries, no serious break had occurred between them, as was to occur later. This bureaucracy comprised a body of professional officeholders, career men who felt that they were particularly competent to run the government. They favored keeping the cabinet responsible to the emperor, because they, as technical experts, could then advise the emperor to keep the cabinet filled with men from their own class.

The party politicians, on the other hand, favored making the cabinet responsible to the Diet rather than to the emperor. Their aim was to attain a government like that of England, where the cabinet is composed of the leaders of the dominant party in Parliament. The party politicians included among their ranks theoretical liberals like the followers of Itagaki, strongly influenced by Rousseau's doctrine of popular sovereignty; practical progressives like the followers of Okuma, who were admirers of the British parliamentary system; and opportunists of no principles who merely wanted to capture for themselves the offices held by the bureaucrats.[9]

Aside from the fact that the bureaucrats wanted to hang on to the power which they possessed and that the party politi-

---

[9] Paul H. Clyde, *A History of the Modern and Contemporary Far East* (New York, 1936), pp. 275–276.

cians wanted to supplant them, there was no essential difference of policy between the two. Domestically, both groups favored continued modernization and reforms. Their ends were the same; the question was merely one of speed. The bureaucrats, better trained technically, wisely tried to make haste slowly, while the politicians, unencumbered by any responsibility, clamored for the immediate attainment of the millennium.[10] In foreign policy, also, there was no essential conflict over issues except on minor points, for Japan's timid and tentative excursions into imperialism were still of a modest and unambitious character.[11] Furthermore, both the bureaucrats and the party politicians were recruited primarily from the same social and economic class, namely, the gentry or the upper middle class. The higher aristocrats were merely impotent social ornaments, and the masses were still inarticulate. Owing to this lack of real issues and to their common social background, the bureaucrats and the party politicians managed to avoid a showdown fight. The Genro, or so-called Elder Statesmen, representing the leadership of the bureaucracy, generally managed to be the power behind the throne, taking the party politicians into a limited sort of partnership with them whenever necessary to prevent them from blocking the government altogether.[12]

[10] J. H. Gubbins, *The Making of Modern Japan* (London, 1922), pp. 157–158.
[11] As evidenced by the comparative absence of parliamentary criticism of the government's foreign policy until the outburst of censure in the Thirty-sixth Diet in 1915 over the handling of the Twenty-one Demands. See Tatsuji Takeuchi, *War and Diplomacy in the Japanese Empire* (New York, 1935), pp. 191–193.
[12] Harold S. Quigley, *Japanese Government and Politics* (New York, 1932), pp. 209–211.

The Renaissance of Asia

The struggle for power became vastly more complicated and dangerous, however, during and after the World War period, for elements other than the bureaucrats and the old line party politicians began to make a bid for control. The underlying cause of this new complexity in politics was the change in the fundamental economy of the country stimulated by the World War. Europe's preoccupation with the war gave Japan an opportunity to supplant the European nations as the chief producer for the markets of the Orient and Oceania, with the result that Japan's industry and commerce grew by leaps and bounds. For the first time, industry came to overshadow agriculture as the mainstay of the nation's economy.[18]

The European war, although it helped to bring about the maturing of Japanese industry at just this time, was not, however, the basic cause for the industrialization itself. The process of industrialization had started much earlier and was rooted deep in the natural conditions of the country. As is well known, Japan is a small country, about the size of California, and more than 80 per cent of its area is rugged mountains. On this limited area lived a population which, by the time of the World War, already numbered more than 50 millions and was increasing at the rate of about 900 thousands each year. Agriculture was obviously incapable of supporting this growing population.

Now this problem of a population pressure was not a problem unique to Japan, nor was the Japanese birth rate

[18] Cf. Kokujiro Yamasaki and Gotaro Ogawa, *Effects of the World War upon the Commerce and Industry of Japan* (New Haven, 1929).

Kawai: Japan

abnormally high for a country in her stage of economic development. A rapid increase in population seems to be a characteristic of all countries during a certain stage in their economic and social development, and Japan was merely following the standard pattern. Europe went through the same process when her population, after having remained virtually stationary for centuries, suddenly doubled in the 18th century and then trebled in the 19th century, only to reach an equilibrium in our own day. Japan was now, a century or two later, going through the same process as Europe.[14] But the adjustments to be made by Japan were much more difficult. Europe had disposed of her growing population by sending her people overseas to colonize distant continents and by harnessing to industry the people who remained, so that with the profits of the sale of manufactured goods she could buy from overseas the foodstuffs which she could no longer grow in sufficient abundance at home. When, however, the population pressure approached the acute stage in Japan, colonization abroad was no longer possible, because all the empty spaces of the world had already been staked out by the Europeans. Industrialization also was difficult, for the markets of the world were already preëmpted by the older industrialized nations, and furthermore Japan lacked the raw materials such as coal, iron, and petroleum which an industrialized society demands.[15] Birth control was not a practical solution, for although it might be the ultimate solution in the long run,

---

[14] Cf. W. R. Crocker, *The Japanese Population Problem* (London, 1931), particularly ch. iv.
[15] John E. Orchard, *Japan's Economic Position* (New York, 1930), pp. 26–48.

there had already been born in Japan during the preceding decade or two, millions of children who would soon be demanding employment. Not fewer than 250 thousand new jobs had to be created every year to take care of those already born.[16]

Of the possible solutions, industrialization, difficult as it was under the peculiar circumstances confronting Japan, was unquestionably the only feasible one.[17] So, through diligent effort and the fortuitous assistance given by the World War, Japanese industry finally managed to come into its own. Industrial development for a time then satisfactorily alleviated the population pressure. Increase in industrial production more than kept pace with the population growth, with the result that Japan for a time experienced unprecedented prosperity. During the decade following the World War, the annual national income increased by six times; the national wealth increased three and a half times; the per capita consumption of rice increased by 20 per cent; the per capita consumption of fish more than doubled.[18] In spite of the growing population, the people came to have more to eat, better things to wear, more of everything that made life pleasant, than ever before in history. The Japanese standard of living, higher than that of any other country of the Orient to start with, became higher than ever. Swarms of taxis filled the streets; beer parlors and cafés sprang up like mushrooms; joyous throngs flocked to the dance halls. The native habit of thrift

---

[16] Teijiro Uyeda, *Future of the Japanese Population* (Tokyo, 1933), p. 12.
[17] Orchard, *op. cit.*, p. 48.
[18] Crocker, *op. cit.*, pp. 53–62.

Kawai: Japan

and the puritanical virtues retreated as the glamorously exotic thrills and sins imported from the West came within the easy reach of the purses of the masses for the first time; and the jazz age struck Japan with full force.[19]

Although the industrialization of the country brought prosperity and a temporary postponement of the problem of overpopulation, it also brought new problems of appalling difficulty. Whereas the predominantly agricultural Japan of the prewar days could in the economic sense live a life pretty much unto herself, industrialized Japan found herself precariously dependent upon a multitude of factors rooted in foreign conditions over which she had no control. Her very life depended on her industries, but her industries depended on foreign markets and upon raw materials brought from across the seas. With her principal market in a politically unstable country like China, with her important raw materials like iron, petroleum, cotton, and wool obtainable only from distant countries like America, India, and Australia, Japan found herself in a highly vulnerable position. Furthermore, in spite of the fact that Japan's commerce in her most successful year amounted to less than 4 per cent of the total commerce of the world, her older established competitors sought to stifle her with discriminatory tariff barriers. What assurance was there, then, that Japanese industry could go on taking care of the growing population for the thirty or forty years which must yet pass before natural factors should

---

[19] The Japanese coined the word *ero-gro* to characterize the tendency of this period, the term being derived from the English words "erotic" and "grotesque," qualities which particularly marked the Japanese version of the jazz age.

76 The Renaissance of Asia

bring about the predicted cessation of Japan's population growth?[20]

In addition to the problem of continuing this delicately maintained industry, industrialization brought grave social problems to disturb the country. It caused the rise of a powerful industrial plutocracy, a Japanese counterpart of Wall Street, greedy for more power. It created an urban proletariat with all the social ills attendant upon the too rapid growth of this class as millions of workers, lured by the bountiful wages paid by expanding industry, flocked from the countryside into the great industrial cities. It created dangerous unrest and discontent among the forgotten peasantry, whose condition, although actually no worse than before, seemed unjustly poor in comparison with the relative prosperity of the industrial workers. And for many, city life in the industrial centers, emancipated too suddenly from the traditional patterns of Japanese life, bred a spirit of irresponsibility and selfish pleasure-seeking, a weakening of the moral fiber. These new problems raised issues which dwarfed into insignificance the old political rivalry between the bureaucrats and the party politicians, and new rivalries based on the clashing class interests of the groups created by industrialization came to dominate the perennial struggle for the control of the throne which characterizes Japanese politics.[21]

---

[20] Cf. Uyeda, *op. cit., passim*, for the calculations of several authorities on population problems, indicating that the population of Japan would become stationary in about three decades. See also Crocker, *op. cit.;* and E. F. Penrose, *Population Theories and Their Application, with Particular Reference to Japan* (Stanford University, 1934).

[21] Cf. Malcolm D. Kennedy, *The Changing Fabric of Japan* (London, 1930), *passim*.

Kawai: Japan

The first of the new groups to make a bid for political power was the industrial plutocracy,[22] which for a while swept everything before it. Lavishly using their financial strength, the industrial interests completely captured the old line party machines. For example, in one election a single corporation was reputed to have contributed 3 million yen to the campaign fund of a particular party.[23] The industrial interests also corralled the support of the urban proletariat through their advocacy of political democracy. Although the ultimate interests of big business and of the proletariat were in opposition and although big business certainly did not favor social or economic democracy, it did favor political democracy, because a politically active proletariat would be a valuable tool so long as it could be properly herded by the party machines now safely in the employ of plutocracy. Hence, the industrialists aided the masses in securing universal manhood suffrage over the opposition of the bureaucracy,[24] and even conceded to the masses some social legislation of a fairly advanced character.[25] Confronted by this disconcerting spectacle of plutocracy leading the masses, bureaucracy capitulated, and by 1918 party government came to prevail with the cabinet virtually responsible to a Diet packed with the hirelings of big busi-

---

[22] No fine discrimination in terminology will be made between industry, finance, and commerce, for in Japan these terms are practically interchangeable inasmuch as the same men control and represent all three.

[23] The Mitsui interests and the Seiyukai party.

[24] Clyde, *op. cit.*, p. 599.

[25] For example, the thoroughgoing revision in 1923 of the Factory Law of 1916 and its effective application since 1926; the repeal in 1926 of the restrictive Labor Law of 1900; etc. See Harold G. Moulton, *Japan: An Economic and Financial Appraisal* (Washington, 1931), pp. 349 ff.

ness.[26] The gentlemen bureaucrats, reduced to the position of errand boys for the political parties, which in turn were controlled by moneyed interests, salvaged what influence they could by allowing the *nouveau riche* industrialists to marry into their select social circle. Thus there resulted a complete merger of bureaucracy, machine politics, and big business.[27]

This combination held this dominant position virtually throughout the decade of the 1920's. It did not matter which of the two major parties was in office, or whether, in the absence of a clear majority, bureaucrats who held the balance of power between the parties formed coalition or "national" cabinets, for inasmuch as they were all now allied with big business through financial or marriage connections, it made no difference.

During the period of its control over the government, big business at first experimented heavily with an imperialistic policy, as evidenced by the Twenty-one Demands served upon China in 1915 and the intervention in Siberia in 1918. But these imperialistic adventures backfired.[28] Businessmen quickly learned that customers could be held only by cultivating their good will, and that to dig raw materials out with bayonets cost far more than to buy them through peaceful trade. By the early 1920's the industrial and commercial classes consequently became ardent converts to the idea of international peace and coöperation and free trade, not out of ideal-

---

[26] Clyde, *op. cit.*, pp. 596–598.
[27] Cf. Harold M. Vinacke, *A History of the Far East in Modern Times* (New York, 2d edition, revised, 1936), pp. 490–492.
[28] Takeuchi, *op. cit.*, pp. 183–195, 204–218.

ism but out of practical considerations.²⁹ Thus there resulted a violent break between the glory-at-any-price militarists and the profit-computing industrialists who now adopted the tactics of International Rotary handshakings and Chamber of Commerce good-will tours. This is the seemingly paradoxical fact which foreigners fail so often to understand: that in Japan, since the early 1920's, capitalism and militaristic imperialism have not gone hand in hand; that big business stands for peace and international coöperation and the profits to be derived therefrom, while a militaristic policy is pushed by the elements that oppose capitalistic industry.

Under the control of big business, Baron Shidehara, apostle of international reasonableness and friendliness, came to preside over the Foreign Office.³⁰ Business-dominated cabinets recalled the armies from the continent,³¹ agreed to the Washington naval disarmament treaties,³² disbanded four divisions of the army and put the remainder on reduced strength,³³ forced the outraged navy to accept the London naval disarmament agreement,³⁴ and rushed through by steam-roller tactics the ratification of the Kellogg Peace Pact.³⁵ When British and American gunboats bombarded the rampaging Chinese troops at Nanking in 1927, the Japanese not only refused the

---
²⁹ Hosea Ballou Morse and Harley Farnsworth MacNair, *Far Eastern International Relations* (Boston, 1931), pp. 771–773.
³⁰ Roy Hidemichi Akagi, *Japan's Foreign Relations* (Tokyo, 1936), pp. 394 ff.
³¹ Morse and MacNair, *op. cit.*, p. 664.
³² Takeuchi, *op. cit.*, pp. 227–238.
³³ Yoshitaro Takenobu (ed.), *The Japan Year Book, 1930* (Tokyo, 1930), pp. 134–135.
³⁴ Takeuchi, *op. cit.*, pp. 283 336. ³⁵ *Ibid.*, pp. 262–274.

invitation to join in, but rather conspicuously shed tears of sympathy for their abused Chinese brethren.[36] This was peace and good will with a vengeance.

Laudable and desirable though the attitude of big business was with respect to foreign relations, its monopolistic control of politics at home was marked by grave abuses. Its control in the first place rested upon the corruption of politics—upon buying out all the politicians. When a candidate for a seat in parliament spent 60,000 yen for campaign expenses when the position paid a salary of about one-twentieth of the amount, it was obvious that no one could afford the luxury of a political career unless he was a plutocrat himself or had the backing of the plutocrats.[37] Although big business stood for political liberalism, it was political liberalism of the sort that allowed the powerful to do what they pleased without restraint. It favored rugged individualism of the type which gave the little man freedom to pit his strength individually and without intervention against the giant corporations. Small businesses were pressed to the wall, and an increasing proportion of the nation's economic activities came under the control of a small group of bankers. Through dummy corporations, holding companies, and interlocking directorates, eight families came to control more than 50 per cent of all Japanese trade and industry. One family, the Mitsui, came to possess 15 per

---

[36] Akagi, *op. cit.*, p. 396.

[37] The Electoral Law of 1925 stipulated that the campaign expenses of each candidate should not exceed .40 yen per franchise holder in each electoral district, which allowed approximately 12,000 to 15,000 yen per candidate. It is an open secret, however, that the hidden expenses of some candidates reached 60,000 yen. Cf. Takenobu, *op. cit.*, p. 71.

cent of all the capital in the Empire.[38] In other words, big business stuck its head out invitingly far for the axe of reaction which was bound to fall.

The first signs of reaction against the domination of politics by the financially privileged class were manifested in the activities of the proletarian parties. Although the masses had followed the leadership of the big business interests in the fight for political democracy against bureaucracy, once that fight was over with the capitulation of bureaucracy, the masses turned against big business on the issue of economic democracy. The abuses of the regime of financial power gave the proletarian parties great popularity. The discontented farming class, blaming their misery upon the capitalistic government which aided big business to the neglect of farm relief, joined with the city laborers in their attack upon the corrupt plutocracy. But despite obvious popularity, the proletarian parties failed to win many elections. The financial resources of the business-controlled parties were too much for the proletarians in the expensive election campaigns. Moreover, the proletarians could not coöperate among themselves, for although they were all bitterly anticapitalist, they comprised all shades of views, ranging from those of the theoretical Social Democrats, tinged only with the faintest trace of pink and led by the kindly old Professor Isoh Abe, to those of the outright Communists advocating violent revolution, led by professional agitators directly inspired and financed from Moscow. The masses consequently dissipated their energy conducting

---

[38] "Men, Yen, and Machines," *Fortune*, Vol. 14, No. 3 (September, 1936), p. 127.

bitter ideological controversies among themselves and splitting their votes among a multitude of candidates representing only slight shades of difference in viewpoint. They became disillusioned and disheartened over the apparent futility of their fight against special privilege, and came to question the efficacy of parliamentary methods to attain their objectives.[39]

At this point the army stepped forward to proclaim itself the champion of the masses against the oppression of big business. The army's bitterness toward the financial interests over the abandonment of an imperialistic policy on the continent and the adoption of the policy of international conciliation and coöperation is easy enough to understand. But the naturalness and plausibility of the army's pretension to being the champion of the masses can only be understood by studying the change which had been taking place in the composition of the Japanese army.

Until quite recently, the officer corps of the army had been made up preponderantly of men of the gentry class, the same social class that constituted the old bureaucracy. In the pre-World War days when the bureaucracy ruled the country, the army officers, as the military segment of the bureaucracy, shared the rule with the civilian portion of the bureaucracy. The two belonged to the same social class, they intermarried, there was no distinction between them. When after the World War the industrial plutocracy gained control of the political parties and the political parties in turn began to run the government, bureaucracy, it will be remembered,

[39] For a brief summary of the activities of the proletarian parties, see Clyde, *op. cit.*, pp. 718–720.

had capitulated and had merged with the plutocracy. This merger included the army officers as well as the civilian officials, and for a while the army, like everything else, became subservient to financial power. This was particularly true of the older officers of higher rank, who became intimately associated with the plutocracy. Although they did not show much enthusiasm for plutocracy's peaceful policy, they accepted with fairly good grace the drastic curtailment of the military program and were compensated by being allowed to dip into the fleshpots of industry.[40]

As the gentry and the plutocracy merged, sons of the gentry found increasing opportunities in business and ceased to go into the army as a career. A gentleman no longer became an officer; he became an industrial magnate. The hitherto unprivileged peasant boys and the sons of the lower middle class families then began to snap up the officers' commissions which the sons of gentlemen now spurned, until the lower ranks in the officer corps came to be composed in large measure of men of peasant origin. Naturally they shared the antagonism of the masses toward big business, and they viewed with apprehension the peaceful foreign policy of the merchants which threatened to cramp the opportunities for glorious military careers. With all the enthusiasm of new converts, these peasant officers emphasized the old Spartan virtues of the ancient warrior caste or the samurai, and considered themselves to be their spiritual heirs, while the real blood descendants of the ancient samurai were now succumbing to the decadent luxuries of the moneyed class. Finally, when

---
[40] Vinacke, *op. cit.*, p. 491.

these younger officers rose to positions of importance in the army, they overrode their superannuated aristocratic superiors and stepped forward to proclaim themselves as the liberators of the nation from the oppression of corrupt capitalistic government.[41]

These army officers, being not too intelligent outside of their specialty of guns and mathematics, have no clear-cut program of social and political reorganization. But in a vague sort of way they stand for the overthrow of capitalistic industry and the establishment of some sort of state socialism. They proclaim that their aim was to free the emperor from the clutches of the greedy capitalists who had made themselves the power behind the throne.

In matters of foreign policy, these military men assert that the peace-at-any-price capitalists have, for the sake of their own immediate profit, betrayed the best interest of the nation. How can the future of the country be safe when the markets for Japanese goods are at the mercy of tariff arrangements of countries over which Japan has no influence? How can Japan's industries be sure of a permanent supply of raw materials when they may be cut off at any time at the whim of some distant country? How can we put our faith in the continuance of coöperation on the part of strange countries that pass discriminatory racial legislation and needlessly irri-

---

[41] For a brief summary of the rise of Japanese "fascism," see Clyde, *op. cit.*, pp. 723–727. See also Vinacke, *op. cit.*, pp. 492–496; T. A. Bisson, "The Rise of Fascism in Japan," *Foreign Policy Reports*, October 26, 1932; Kenneth W. Colegrove, *Militarism in Japan* (Boston, 1936); Emil Lederer, "Fascist Tendencies in Japan," *Pacific Affairs*, Vol. 7, No. 4 (December, 1934), pp. 373–385.

tating immigration laws against our people and insist on binding us to an inferior naval ratio when their superior navies make themselves at home in more than one ocean far from their homelands? How can we be satisfied with the scant leavings of countries which have staked out more of the world than they need and have then adopted a dog-in-the-manger attitude toward all newcomers?

The only security for Japan's future, say these military men, is for Japan to create a self-sufficing economic bloc of nations, within easy reach and influence of Japan, which will supply Japan with raw materials and which will consume Japanese manufactures. Such economic coöperation between Japan and her very close neighbors would be mutually beneficial, and these neighbors should be glad to enter into such arrangements voluntarily, but if through unintelligence or perversity or through the machinations of distant interferers they refuse to coöperate, Japan should go ahead anyway and set up this self-sufficient economic bloc by force. Later, when the blessings of the arrangement become clear, these originally unwilling neighbors will thank Japan for her insistent action. And in this economic block there should be no capitalistic enterprise run for private profit, but only state monopolies run for the benefit of a collective society as a whole. Any other course would be suicide, say the militarists. Foreign criticism and threats of boycott, instead of deterring the militarists, spur them all the more, because they serve only to confirm the conviction that Japan will never be safe until she creates an economically self-sufficient empire.

These claims of the militarists met with violent opposition

from the businessmen; but the common people, the laborers, the farmers, and the small tradesmen were greatly impressed. Here was the army with its prestige and power offering its leadership in the fight against hateful big business. A wholesale desertion from the ineffective proletarian parties to the military-sponsored fascistic state socialism took place. Although the army officers did not know much economics, their intentions were noble, their hands were clean. They might be narrow-minded and misguided, but they were sincere and honest and patriotic. In contrast, the party politicians had more intelligence and sounder ideas with respect both to economics and to foreign policy, but they represented an unpopular, corrupt plutocracy, now accused of being unpatriotic and in league with international interests. Popular opinion was unquestionably swinging toward the army. If anyone was to clean out the Augean stables of corrupt politics, it must be the army, and the public gave it their blessing. The army, thus strengthened by public support, went to work.[42]

The actions of the army since 1931 are recent history which needs no detailed recounting.[43] Taking advantage of the Manchurian incident and the ensuing perpetual crisis with China, the army tugged at its leash and dragged the government after it. Yet even under wartime conditions the army has failed to gain complete control. The old political parties con-

---

[42] William Henry Chamberlain, *Japan Over Asia* (Boston, 1937), *passim*, explains graphically the contrast in views between the industrialists and the militarists.

[43] For a brief summary see Clyde, *op. cit.*, pp. 727–734; Vinacke, *op. cit.*, pp. 495–502.

tinued to win all the elections, and it was difficult to tell from the returns whether the electorate supported the old line parties out of disapproval of the army's too active foreign policy, or whether it was merely proof that the old party machines were still functioning too completely under the thumb of big business in spite of popular support for the army. The extremist section of the army, being convinced that the latter was true, then resorted to direct action, and there followed the wholesale assassination by military men of party politicians on May 15, 1932, and the unsuccessful attempt at a *coup d'état* to establish a military dictatorship on February 26, 1936.

In the face of these assaults the surprising thing is not that Japan is as fascistically inclined as she is, but that she has so stubbornly resisted a complete military dictatorship as long as she has. The government is gradually being coerced in the direction of a military-dominated national socialistic state, to be sure, but at the present moment Japan is still quite far from being an out-and-out military dictatorship. Although she is superficially grouped with Italy and Germany, Japan is still far short of the authoritarianism of those dictatorships. Parliamentary government still functions, although with increasing deference to the pressure groups sympathetic to the army. Parliamentarism may be not much more than mere form, but the tenaciousness with which the form persists is significant. The explanation is that neither side desires a showdown, for neither is sure of complete victory. Although there is no likelihood that a reversal of trend will occur within the predictable future, so as to allow a democratic liberal

88 The Renaissance of Asia

regime to come into power, the failure of the military *putsch* of 1936 warned the military men that the nation still would not tolerate a complete dictatorship. The result has been, within recent years, a succession of short-lived cabinets representing makeshifts and uneasy compromises including both the civilian moderates and the military extremists, but with the balance of power swinging increasingly toward the militarists.

Many foreigners would believe that the struggle in Japan is a clear-cut issue between a liberal, democratic, peaceful civilian element and a reactionary, imperialistic military clique. The issue unfortunately is not so simple as that. The elements that stand for peace and moderation in foreign affairs stand for special privilege and exploitation of the masses at home. The elements that champion the underdog at home stand for a well-intentioned but dangerously vigorous policy abroad. Both sides are being propelled by great social forces over which individuals have little control.

It might even be more reassuring and desirable if an autocratic emperor and a few powerful advisers could sit in council and arbitrarily chart the course of the Empire, for then there would at least be conscious direction. But, contrary to general belief, the Japanese government, in common with most governments, cannot be managed in that way. The destiny of the Empire and the destiny of the neighbors of the Empire rest upon the outcome of the four-cornered tug of war between the industrialist, the laborer, the farmer, and the soldier, all of them created and moved by social and economic forces which they cannot fully understand or control. In the meantime, a mild-mannered young emperor who would personally much rather play with his microscope and butterfly collection and his private nine-hole golf course in the palace grounds than worry about war or politics, helplessly awaits the outcome of a titanic struggle which ironically is being fought in his name.

JAPAN'S AIMS AND ASPIRATIONS ON THE CONTINENT OF ASIA

N. WING MAH
ASSOCIATE PROFESSOR OF POLITICAL SCIENCE
IN THE UNIVERSITY OF CALIFORNIA

Lecture delivered April 24, 1939

JAPAN'S AIMS AND ASPIRATIONS
ON THE CONTINENT OF ASIA

ANY EXAMINATION of Japan's aims and aspirations on the continent of Asia today would be devoid of clarity if it omitted to delve into the past for historical precedent and to dip into the future for possible repercussions. The present Sino-Japanese War is not the outcome of one isolated "incident" that has exploded without warning, to rend asunder the very foundations of peace in the Far East and reverberate ominously throughout the whole civilized world. Military maneuvers at Lukouchiao (Marco Polo Bridge), about twenty miles southwest of Peiping, where the Japanese had no right to hold them,[1] forged but another link in a chain that has its anchors well imbedded in the past. July 7, 1937, the day on which the present hostilities broke out, marks but the climax of a series of events which have progressed menacingly in only one ultimate direction. War was the inevitable outcome when a nation long faced with the problem of life and death finally accepted the grim conclusion that it could react in only one way. It threw down the gauntlet to the aggressor, and resistance to invasion begot war.

Truly enough has it been said that the foreign policy of any state is irrevocably intertwined with domestic considerations. But whether such domestic factors in Japan have been chiefly economic and social, as opposed to the nationalistic, chauvin-

[1] John V. A. MacMurray, *Treaties and Agreements with and concerning China, 1894–1919* (New York, 1921), Vol. I, pp. 282–283, 317; T. A. Bisson, *Japan in China* (New York, 1938), pp. 12–15; Shuhsi Hsü, *How the Far Eastern War Was Begun* (Shanghai, 1938), ch. ii.

istic, and imperialistic influences which history reveals as having shaped her behavior, is a highly controversial question. Japan could have obtained all the necessary raw materials she desired from China through the peaceful channels of trade and commerce, and it was inevitable that China, with her teeming millions and close proximity to the island empire of Nippon, would have been a prosperous market and outlet for Japanese goods and products. A flourishing trade would have resulted from mutual good will and friendship. China was only too receptive to friendly overtures, not only from Japan, but from all other foreign countries, and would have welcomed constructive assistance in the successful consummation of her work of national rehabilitation and reconstruction. Toward this end she sought the coöperation of the League of Nations, and experts who have been placed at the disposal of the National Economic Council in China have been received with enthusiasm. But Japan has not only consistently and passively withheld her aid; she has actively interfered and hindered at every turn. Particularly during the past decade, when the demands of a modern age pressed relentlessly upon China and rapid strides were made toward national unity, has Japan been incessantly obstructive in forestalling progress, apparently lest chances of subduing China diminish with her political and economic modernization. She recently declared to the world that she would not countenance concerted aid to China "even in the name of financial and technical assistance."[2] Modern China, bent on national recon-

---

[2] Shuhsi Hsü, *The North China Problem* (Shanghai, 1937), pp. 61–73; *The China Year Book, 1934* (Shanghai, 1934), pp. 725–729; George H.

struction and dedicated to a foreign policy of peace and non-aggression with all nations, was never a potential enemy to the security of her island neighbor, but was always a great potential field for legitimate economic enterprise. But it would appear that the economic and social factors—raw materials, population pressure, world markets, and the like—over which Japan has made much ado in recent times are less important than the nationalistic, chauvinistic, and imperialistic factors—dream of empire and lust for conquest—which have long been evident as traditions deeply rooted in her national life.[3]

The dream of a Japanese world empire may be said to have begun with that Japanese military genius and leader of the late 16th century, Toyotomi Hideyoshi. After his brilliant military successes in forcibly bending all the warlike feudal lords in Japan to his will, thereby giving to his country perhaps its first real national unity in history, he aspired to achieve for the glory of Japan a great Asiatic empire.[4] Retaining command of a vast army of veterans, he planned the grandiose foreign venture that would make Japan the mistress of the whole Asiatic world.[5] His plans embraced China, Korea, India, Persia, and other Asiatic nations within the ken of Japan. Nor were the islands along the Asiatic coast, Liu Chiu, For-

Blakeslee, *Conflicts of Policy in the Far East* (New York, 1934), pp. 22–24; Harold S. Quigley and George H. Blakeslee, *The Far East* (Boston, 1938), pp. 90–92, 190–191, 285–290.

[3] Robert T. Pollard, "Dynamics of Japanese Imperialism," *Pacific Historical Review*, Vol. 8; No. 1 (March, 1939), pp. 7–17.

[4] G. B. Sansom, *Japan: A Short Cultural History* (New York, 1936), pp. 401–405; Payson J. Treat, *The Far East* (New York, 1935), p. 283.

[5] Yoshi S. Kuno, *Japanese Expansion on the Asiatic Continent* (Berkeley, 1937), Vol. 1, ch. iv.

96 The Renaissance of Asia

mosa, and the Philippines, and other islands in the South Sea, to be overlooked. His idea was to establish his ruling authority effectively over China, Japan, and Korea, together with the neighboring islands, as the first unit of his continental empire, with Peking, instead of Kyoto, as Japan's imperial capital.[6] He proposed first the conquest of China, using the kingdom of Korea, which he held in haughty contempt, as the highroad into China.[7] In 1592 he launched his foreign expedition into Korea, and that country became a virtual doormat for the trampling feet of his fierce warriors on their way to the farther goal of China. However, Hideyoshi's carefully nourished military undertaking fell short of his lofty ambitions. For six war-torn years Korea refused the "coöperation" demanded of her.[8] The Korean peninsula was brutally and thoroughly ravaged from end to end, a treatment which won for the Japanese nation not the submission expected of the Koreans, but their undying hatred.[9] Far from achieving his aims, which envisaged a triumphant entry into Peking, the capital of China, at the close of the year 1592,[10] this Japanese imperialist of the 16th century found that his projected continental conquest had become a protracted war confined almost entirely to Korea.

In 1598, after a brief lull in hostilities, Hideyoshi once more made a vigorous thrust on China from Korea, but again he was repulsed. It was to be his last attempt, however, for death

---

[6] *Ibid.*, pp. 143, 147.
[7] Kenneth S. Latourette, *The Development of Japan* (New York, 1936), p. 64; Pollard, *op. cit.*, p. 18.
[8] Kuno, *op. cit.*, pp. 144–145. [10] Kuno, *op. cit.*, p. 147.
[9] Latourette, *op. cit.*, p. 64.

suddenly overtook him in that year. The invading legions of Japan were compelled to retreat, and to return home with no booty of war. Thus came to an inglorious end, in the closing years of the 16th century, Hideyoshi's dream of empire and Japan's quest for world glory in Asia.

In spite of this early frustration at continental expansion, however, the lust for conquest as envisaged by Hideyoshi did not die with him. His exploits had temporarily collapsed, but at some opportune time in the future the national desire for their revival and reënactment was destined to be reawakened.

In the meantime, after Hideyoshi's death and the subsequent rise of the feudal clan of the Tokugawa under Iyeyasu to the exalted position of *de facto* rulership in Japan, no foreign venture of any kind was undertaken and the country lived in a state of self-imposed isolation during a long unbroken period. Following the retirement of Hideyoshi's invading hordes from the Korean peninsula, "until modern times Japan abandoned hopes of foreign conquest, as well she might, since this one overseas adventure had lasted six years and had cost her in vain many lives and much treasure."[11] Tokugawa Iyeyasu and his successors found it expedient to concentrate upon establishing firmly the governing power of the Tokugawa and to insure its indefinite perpetuation. To that end they labored successfully;[12] for some 254 years Japan enjoyed an unprecedented era of peace. Before the decline of the ruling Tokugawa shoguns Old Japan was at her best, with internal development of national life uninterrupted by any distracting external influences. This peculiar state of af-

---
[11] Sansom, *op. cit.*, p. 405. [12] *Ibid.*, pp. 433–444.

98   The Renaissance of Asia

fairs obtaining in Japan must also be explained partly by the fact that, since the arrival of the first Portuguese trading fleet at Canton in 1517, European traders and others confined primarily to China their interest and activities in exploring the possibilities of trade and profit. It was, moreover, the tales of the fabulous wealth of China, not that of Japan, that originally attracted the Europeans to the Orient. Until the second quarter of the 19th century, European interest in Japan was practically nil.

In 1853, however, the seclusion of Japan was abruptly challenged and invaded by the extension of American interests in the Pacific and the Far East.[13] But even then, for a period of more than ten years after the first treaty with America was signed,[14] Japan did not cease to resent the influx of the West upon her shores.[15] Finally, in 1867, when the downfall of the Tokugawa government at Yedo was precipitated by the reopening of the country to foreign intercourse, and the Mikado was presumably restored to direct rule,[16] Japan reversed her old national policy of isolation and decided to emulate the ways of the Western world. With the advantage of a powerful and privileged ruling class to serve as the impetus of all movements for change and reform, the success of the island empire of Nippon was phenomenal. Moreover, since this ruling class, the samurai, was a highly trained military caste—military in spirit, outlook and tradition,—Japan had every incentive to

---

[13] Tyler Dennet, *Americans in Eastern Asia* (New York, 1922), pp. 249–264; Foster R. Dulles, *America in the Pacific* (Boston, 1932), ch. v.

[14] March 31, 1854.

[15] J. H. Gubbins, *The Making of Modern Japan* (London, 1922), pp. 53–59.

[16] Wm. McGovern, *Modern Japan* (New York, 1920), p. 47.

Mah: Japan

adapt herself readily to military and naval modernization as a first requisite to national power and security. She was quick to see that the weapons, methods, and tactics used by Western nations to pry open her gates would prove useful in the furtherance of her own national glory.[17] The frenzied zeal of Japan for national power like that of the newcomers of the West contributed in no small measure to redoubled efforts in a military and naval expansion that was to result in her meteoric elevation to the status of a world power with an active voice in international power politics. With the philosophy of force fundamentally dominant in the character of the ruling class, it was no impossible feat to transform a chauvinistic race into a nation at once militaristic and imperialistic.[18] The hostility against the foreigner, and the effort to match and surpass the strength that stood behind the scientific civilization of the West, spurred the movements for reform. And let it be said in passing that even to this day the antagonism toward the foreigner persists and reasserts itself articulately in increasingly numerous ways.[19] For with all its apparent rapid modernization the Japanese nation has remained essentially unchanged in ideology and attitude. Traditional Japan has been left undisturbed in character and spirit, and any antiquated practice of the past is freely utilized so long as it accelerates the rise of the state to world power. The institution of emperor worship, based on his alleged divinity, has been built up by all imaginable kinds of artifice into a potent politico-religious

---

[17] Latourette, *op. cit.*, pp. 81–82.
[18] Kenneth W. Colegrove, *Militarism in Japan* (Boston, 1936), pp. 5–7; Latourette, *op. cit.*, p. 82.
[19] McGovern, *op. cit.*, p. 42.

cult, which serves as the principal fount and generator of Japanese patriotism, nationalism, and imperialism.[20] Manifest destiny is a national credo constantly kept alive by this exaltation of the prestige and glory of the Mikado and his empire.

While the nation was faced with the task of coping with the requirements of a new age, the Hideyoshi tradition of world empire was resuscitated. Yoshida Shoin of Choshiu is credited with being the bold spirit who first openly advocated the resumption of Japanese expansion on the Asiatic mainland and islands.[21] He was one of those restless samurai who fretted under the Tokugawa policy of seclusion, and when the regime fell into decay and the national life, socially, economically, and spiritually, became seriously demoralized, he clamored for adventure. He limited, however, the expansion of Japan to the acquisition of Kamchatka, the Kurile Islands, the Liu Chiu Islands, Formosa, and Manchuria on the mainland; and he demanded tribute of Korea. This restriction to a narrower scope of oversea expansion was probably due in part to the appearance of powerful Western nations in the Far East and in part to the fact that Japan was at that time wading through a period of internal weakness. There was no question that the circumstances of his time were radically different from those when Hideyoshi was at his prime. Nevertheless, Yoshida Shoin, through his persistent efforts to resurrect the national glory of the past and to attain for his country a comparable international status, gave great impetus to the

---

[20] McGovern, *op. cit.*, pp. 124–132; Colegrove, *op. cit.*, pp. 7–10.

[21] See Iichiro Tokutomi, "The Life of Yoshida Shoin" (translated by H. E. Coleman), *Transactions of the Asiatic Society of Japan*, Vol. 45 (Pt. I, 1917), pp. 119–188.

Mah: Japan

renewal of the movement for a Japanese empire abroad. His premature death at the hands of the Tokugawa government at Yedo in 1859 for traitorous activities in other connections[22] did not blot out his teachings; for the samurai leaders of the "imperial restoration" of 1867–68, among whom were many of his notable disciples,[23] became powerful and influential figures in the making of modern Japan and the gradual delineation of her self-ordained imperial destiny. They preached his gospel and carried on the torch of imperial expansion.[24]

Thus it was that after the overthrow of the Tokugawa shogunate and the rise to supreme political power of the southwestern clans—Satsuma, Choshiu, Hizen, and Tosa—the hand of Japan immediately stretched out into neighboring and outlying lands and islands, and in other ways sought to extend Japanese power and influence abroad.[25] Hardly had the restoration government become securely established when, in 1871, the demand for war on Korea was loudly raised by the samurai.[26] But men like Iwakura, Kido, Okubo, and Ito intervened on the grounds that war was premature and politically inexpedient because the country had just been initiated into an important stage of national transition, finances were at a low ebb, and there was the risk of foreign complications.[27]

---

[22] W. W. McLaren, *A Political History of Japan during the Meiji Era, 1867–1912* (New York, 1916), p. 35.

[23] Inouye Kaoru, Ito Hirobumi, Kido Takayoshi, Saigo Takamori, Yamagata Aritomo.

[24] E. E. N. Causton, *Militarism and Foreign Policy in Japan* (London, 1936), pp. 37–39.

[25] Latourette, *op. cit.*, pp. 149–153.

[26] Gubbins, *op. cit.*, p. 121.

[27] H. B. Morse and H. F. MacNair, *Far Eastern International Relations* (Boston, 1931), p. 387.

The Renaissance of Asia

While a war on Korea was avoided, Japan turned her attention to China. She wanted a privileged position in China, comparable to that obtained by Western powers. That she did succeed in negotiating an equal and reciprocal treaty with China in 1873 apparently did not satisfy her.[28] In 1874 a Japanese expeditionary force was sent to Formosa, ostensibly for the purpose of punishing the Formosan aborigines for the death of several Japanese subjects who were supposed to have been killed when shipwrecked off the island with a group of natives from the Liu Chiu Islands in 1871. Japan failed to obtain possession of Formosa, but she won an indemnity and the opportunity of extending, in 1879, her sovereignty over the Liu Chiu Islands.[29]

In the north Japan contested with Russia over the island of Sakhalin, laying claim to possession on the grounds that Japanese fishermen had settled there. She eventually gained possession of the Kurile Islands in exchange for her claim to Sakhalin in 1875. In 1876, owing to a fracas between Koreans and Japanese sailors in Korean waters, she successfully imposed a treaty on that kingdom which marked "the beginning of her subjugation to Japan"[30] and once more paved the way for Japanese expansion on the Asiatic mainland.[31] For an extended period of time in the past Korea had been an acknowledged vassal of China, and for at least two centuries

---
[28] T. F. Tsiang, *Documents concerning China's Recent Foreign Relations* (Shanghai, 1934), Vol. 2, pp. 59–60. (In Chinese.)
[29] Roy H. Akagi, *Japan's Foreign Relations, 1542–1936* (Tokyo, 1936), p. 60.
[30] Stanley K. Hornbeck, *Contemporary Politics in the Far East* (New York, 1916), p. 199.
[31] Morse and MacNair, *op. cit.*, p. 389.

immediately preceding this modern epoch the continuity of Chinese suzerainty had never been disturbed. Japan now disputed this political relationship and sought control of the peninsula, which was of strategic importance to China. Strained relations between the two countries finally assumed a violent aspect in 1894 when both contestants undertook to dispatch troops to Korea on the occasion of a domestic rebellion there, following which, as a result of mutual disagreement over the question of military withdrawal, hostilities were precipitated. In 1894 the first Sino-Japanese war of modern times began. China under the decadent Manchu regime was no match for her enemy, and in 1895 the positive policy of Japanese military preparedness won a signal victory over the unpreparedness of her weak continental neighbor. China was evicted from Korea, and Japan acquired as spoils of war Formosa, the Pescadores Islands, the Liaotung Peninsula, and a sizable war indemnity, in addition to securing a privileged status in China on an equal footing with the Western powers.[82] Besides materially satisfying the clamor at home for the conquest of Korea, the war of 1894-95 pushed forward the realization of Japan's Asiatic ambitions.

But at this point Japan received an unexpected check. Because she, too, had coveted it, Russia, with the support of France and Germany, demanded the retrocession of the Liaotung Peninsula to China.[83] Japan was forced to comply, but received as compensation from China a sum of 30,000,000 Kuping taels.

[82] E. T. Williams, *A Short History of China* (New York, 1928), p. 363.
[83] Gubbins, *op. cit.*, p. 225.

The Renaissance of Asia

Finally, in February, 1904, Russia and Japan came to blows. The two countries resorted to force to settle their bitter feud developing out of a stubborn contest for political paramountcy in the Korean peninsula. It was as much a war of expansion on the part of Japan as on that of Russia.[84] The dispute also involved the Russian status in Manchuria. Taking advantage of the occasion provided by the Boxer Rebellion of 1900, Russia had moved large contingents of her troops into Manchuria, where, from all indications at the time, she was prepared not only to consolidate her position, but to expand from this vantage point into Korea, which Japan now cherished as her own special sphere. In a word, therefore, the Russo-Japanese War may be described as the result of a counterchallenge hurled by Japan at the potential ascendancy of Russia in Manchuria in retaliation for the original challenge flung at her own desired political supremacy in Korea. Japan moved victoriously on land and sea. Russia was forced out of Korea; Russian rights in southern Manchuria, including the lease of the Liaotung Peninsula which was wrested from China in 1898, were transferred to Japan, thus providing for the future extension of her power and influence into China;[85] and the southern half of the island of Sakhalin was also ceded to her. Japan lost no time in intrenching herself in southern Manchuria, and in 1910 she annexed Korea.

Japan's continental gains from 1875 to 1910—a period of thirty-five years—were a far cry from the extensive conquests

---
[84] McLaren, *op. cit.*, p. 5; Stephen King-Hall, *Western Civilization and the Far East* (New York, 1924), p. 48.
[85] A. M. Pooley, *Japan's Foreign Policies* (London, 1920), pp. 46, 138.

mapped out by Hideyoshi. Radically altered conditions in the Far East within this period, and particularly since the turn of the 20th century, when major Western powers appeared in force on the Far Eastern scene, prevented Japan from exercising freedom of action; but she merely bided her time and waited for more favorable auspices under which to advance her expansionist policy step by step. In the meantime she did not relax in strengthening her position. After recovering her jurisdictional and fiscal independence by aggressive diplomacy in the years 1894-1899, she became an ally of Great Britain by means of the Anglo-Japanese Alliance of 1902.[36] Besides the renewal of this alliance in 1905,[37] she further obtained, following her victory over Russia, important political agreements with France in 1907,[38] with Russia in 1907,[39] with the United States in 1908,[40] with Russia again in 1910,[41] with Great Britain in a third renewal of their joint alliance in 1911,[42] with Russia once more in 1912,[43] and finally with Russia in close alliance in 1916[44]—all of which accorded her full recognition of her new international status, not alone as the foremost power in the Far East, but also as one of the world powers. Thus equipped, she not only maintained the vantage ground previously won, but was established in a strategic position to thwart any open or covert interference with the execution of her continental policy from bases in Korea and southern Manchuria.[45]

[36] MacMurray, *op. cit.*, pp. 324-325.
[37] *Ibid.*, pp. 516-518.
[38] *Ibid.*, p. 640.
[39] *Ibid.*, pp. 657-658.
[40] *Ibid.*, pp. 769-770.
[41] *Ibid.*, pp. 803-804.
[42] *Ibid.*, pp. 900-901.
[43] Williams, *op. cit.*, p. 409.
[44] MacMurray, *op. cit.*, Vol. 2, pp. 1327-1328.
[45] Pooley, *op. cit.*, p. 138.

The Renaissance of Asia

"The opportunity of a myriad years" came to Japan when the World War broke out in Europe in 1914. She evicted Germany from China and the Far East and, jointly with Great Britain, from the Pacific. With all the major powers preoccupied in the world crisis, an international situation was created which Japan utilized without hesitation. She appointed herself overlord of the Far East. By means of the notorious Twenty-one Demands of 1915 she launched her greatest assault on China.[46] Aside from firmly bolstering her position in southern Manchuria and eastern Inner Mongolia, strengthening what she had newly acquired from Germany in Shantung, compelling China to turn over to her virtually all the best Chinese coal and iron resources, and establishing indirect control over China's seacoast, she attempted to foist a Japanese protectorate upon China through the fifth and last group of the Demands. Though she resorted to diplomatic pressure and threats of force, she did not fully succeed.[47] The acceptance of Group Five in its entirety was resisted to the bitter end. Nevertheless, by the treaties and notes of May 25, 1915, she did obtain a firmer hold in China and extorted special privileges[48] which she still insists upon enjoying in China and the Far East. With a free hand in the Far East, Japan lost no time in consolidating her position in Asia.

It should also be noted that Japan had, from the beginning, adopted an obstructive attitude toward the active participation

---

[46] G. Zay Wood, *The Twenty-one Demands* (New York, 1921), chs. i–x; Hornbeck, *op. cit.*, ch. xvii.

[47] *Ibid.*, pp. 326–328.

[48] G. Zay Wood, *The Chino-Japanese Treaties of 1915* (New York, 1921), chs. i–ix, including appendices A–N.

of China in the World War. She had blocked the initiative of China to recover the leasehold of Kiaochow in Shantung in August, 1914.[49] She had further opposed the second attempt of China to join the Allies in August, 1915.[50] Finally, when the Allies continued to press for the active alliance of China, Viscount Ishii issued the following dictum at a conference of Allied ambassadors in Tokyo in November, 1915: "Japan considered developments with regard to China of paramount interest to her ... she must keep a firm hand there. Japan could not regard with equanimity the organization of an efficient Chinese army such as would be required for her active participation in the war, nor could Japan fail to regard with uneasiness a liberation of the economic activities of a nation of four hundred million people."[51] Ultimately, however, early in 1917, foreseeing the irresistible drift of China to the Allied cause when, following the invitation and example of the United States, China severed relations with Germany[52] and later, in August, on her own initiative, declared war, Japan took steps in her own self-interest. She was not to be denied the full benefits accruing to her from the war. In February and March, 1917, she secured secret agreements from Great Britain, Russia, France, and Italy, respectively,[53] wherein provisions were inserted acknowledging the priority of Japanese claims in the Far East and the Pacific and promis-

[49] Paul S. Reinsch, *An American Diplomat in China* (Garden City, 1922), p. 123; Williams, *op. cit.*, pp. 487, 515; Pooley, *op. cit.*, p. 148.

[50] Williams, *op. cit.*, p. 516.

[51] Thomas F. Millard, *Democracy and the Eastern Question* (New York, 1919), p. 99; Williams, *op. cit.*, p. 516.

[52] MacMurray, *op. cit.*, Vol. 2, pp. 1368–1370; Williams, *op. cit.*, p. 518.

[53] *Ibid.*, pp. 519–520; MacMurray, *op. cit.*, Vol. 2, pp. 1167–1169.

ing their diplomatic support of such claims, among others, at the final peace settlement. In return, Japan promised the Allies to encourage the entry of China into the war.[54]

Under the guise of assisting China to participate in the war, therefore, Japanese "international finance" immediately became active in China. Here entered the "Nishihara" and other loans to the "government in power" in Peking, with the support of the Japanese government.[55] Needless to say, the funds were squandered in other directions. Inasmuch as Japan had no genuine desire for China's war participation, China was further tied up militarily by a joint Sino-Japanese military alliance of May, 1918, which, suspiciously enough, permitted Japan, in the event of "military necessity," to dispatch troops to China, particularly to the Manchurian-Siberian border.[56]

When the World War was finally brought to a close, Japanese foreign policy in China received great stimulation at the Paris Peace Conference. When the Treaty of Versailles transferred to Japan all former German rights and privileges in the Chinese province of Shantung, China refused to sign the peace treaty. To entrust to Japan the virtual control of this huge and populous province, of immeasurable strategic[57] and sentimental value to the Chinese people, was interpreted as a direct aspersion upon the principles for which the war had presumably been fought. China had fought a losing diplomatic battle, for her appeal for a review of the Twenty-one Demands of 1915, as well as a readjustment of a series of na-

---

[54] Pooley, *op. cit.*, p. 166; King-Hall, *op. cit.*, pp. 164–166.
[55] Millard, *op. cit.*, pp. 181–193; King-Hall, *op. cit.*, pp. 161–163.
[56] Millard, *op. cit.*, pp. 179–181; Williams, *op. cit.*, pp. 520–521.
[57] Hornbeck, *op. cit.*, p. 346.

Mah: Japan 109

tional grievances,[58] was likewise ignored. But Japan's hopes were heightened, for she profited materially from the War.

Although it has been said by her spokesmen that "Japan's vital issue in foreign affairs is China," the Russian revolution of 1917 created conditions in eastern Siberia which did not fail to attract the immediate attention of Japan. Passing over the question of the so-called threats of Communism and the like, it was not long before the cry of "On to Baikal!" resounded in Japanese military circles. Japanese intervention in eastern Siberia was proposed. It met with disapproval among the Allies; but eventually a joint Siberian intervention was effected in August, 1918, with Japan and the United States as major participants. The latter sent an expeditionary force of 7000, whereas Japan put into eastern Siberia a disproportionately excessive army of more than 70,000. Westward toward Lake Baikal they pushed, with Japanese troops leading the way. In the end, however, the project turned out to be more of a military venture on the part of Japan than an "errand of mercy" for the protection of Allied interests. In January, 1920, the American forces were recalled; those of Japan remained. It was not long before a number of "incidents" occurred, and only the combination of Allied pressure and Russian resistance succeeded in compelling the Japanese army to retire stage by stage to the Russian Maritime Province.[59] When the Washington Conference met in 1921–22, the

[58] *The Shantung Question: A Statement of China's Claim, together with Important Documents Submitted to the Peace Conference in Paris* (San Francisco, 1919).

[59] Williams, *op. cit.*, pp. 533–543; H. K. Norton, *The Far Eastern Republic* (New York, 1923), pp. 113–117; Causton, *op. cit.*, pp. 122–228; King-Hall, *op. cit.*, pp. 207–214.

powers assembled there undertook to become trustees of Russian interests while Russia was in a state of political incompetence.[60] It became incumbent upon Japan to complete the evacuation of her forces, and the last contingent was finally withdrawn in October, 1922.

At the Washington Conference, when the five leading naval powers met on November 11, 1921, to consider the limitation of armaments, a discussion of Pacific and Far Eastern questions was held in connection therewith. As a desirable corollary of the motives which governed the move for naval limitation, the purpose of the discussion, in the words of Secretary of State Hughes, was "to endeavor to reach a common understanding as to the principles and policies to be followed in the Far East" by the powers "and thus greatly to diminish, and if possible wholly to remove, discernible sources of controversy."[61] China was one of the nine invited and participating powers, and she renewed her claims which previously had been rejected at the Paris Peace Conference in 1919. Read in the light of actual conditions prevailing in the Far East, the Treaty of Versailles had virtually ceded the Chinese province of Shantung to Japan. Rectification of this unjust arrangement was demanded of the powers, and under the friendly auspices of the United States and Great Britain an amicable settlement was finally reached outside the Conference.

The outcome of the Washington Conference revealed a

---

[60] *Conference on the Limitation of Armament, Senate Document No. 126*, 67th Congress, 2nd Session (Washington, 1922), pp. 703–707; King-Hall, *op. cit.*, pp. 215–217.

[61] *Conference on the Limitation of Armament*, as cited, p. 42.

new trend in the attitude of the Western powers toward China. A definite embodiment of an enlightened policy looking toward the stabilization of conditions in the Far East and the Pacific area was the new Nine-Power Treaty, wherein the signatories committed themselves to "respect the sovereignty, the independence, and the territorial and administrative integrity of China," and to "provide the fullest and most unembarrassed opportunity to China to develop and maintain for herself an effective and stable government," and reaffirmed the sanctity of the Open Door policy in consonance with such principles. By virtue of this and other agreements adopted at the Conference some measure of peace was brought to Asia, for the imperialistic ambitions of Japan appeared to have been temporarily held in check. Japan did intervene in Chinese internal affairs in 1925[62] and sent troops to Mukden; she also hindered China's national unification movement in 1927 and 1928[63] by dispatching forces into Shantung; and circumstantial evidence bearing upon the assassination of Marshal Chang Tso-lin of Manchuria in 1928 pointed to Japanese involvement.[64] Yet, all in all, it may be said that there was a period of comparative inactivity on the Asiatic mainland from 1922 to 1931.

But it was the lull before the storm. While the world was sunk in the throes of a widespread economic crisis and the problems of unrest which followed in its wake, Japan

---

[62] *League of Nations: Appeal by the Chinese Government, Report of the Commission of Enquiry* (Geneva, 1932) (hereafter cited as *Lytton Report*), p. 28.

[63] *Ibid.*, p. 23; Causton, *op. cit.*, p. 129.

[64] *Lytton Report*, p. 29; A. Morgan Young, *Imperial Japan 1926–1938*, ch. v.

The Renaissance of Asia

scrapped her treaties and dishonored her own signature. When she occupied Mukden in Manchuria on September 18, 1931, she embarked on the first lap of a positive policy of continental expansion.[65] Her entry into Manchuria was but the prelude to an extensively premeditated program of Asiatic conquest that was to stop short of no means, foul or fair, to attain its ends.[66] The attack on Shanghai in January, 1932;[67] the creation of a puppet state in Manchuria in March of the same year;[68] the invasion of the province of Jehol in March, 1933;[69] the establishment of the demilitarized zone in eastern Hopeh in May, 1933;[70] the compulsory restoration of normal relations with Japanese-occupied Manchuria;[71] the Amau "Hands off China" pronouncement of April, 1934;[72] the so-called "Ho-Umetsu Agreement" of June, 1935, seriously infringing upon Chinese authority in North China;[73] the Japanese-instigated North China autonomy movement of November, 1935;[74] the institution of a puppet regime in eastern Hopeh in November, 1935;[75] the further penetration into

---

[65] W. H. Chamberlin, *Japan over Asia* (Boston, 1937), p. 3.

[66] *Lytton Report*, pp. 66–83; P. H. B. Kent, *The Twentieth Century in the Far East* (London, 1937), pp. 253–257.

[67] *Lytton Report*, pp. 84–87.

[68] *Ibid.*, pp. 88–112.

[69] Shuhsi Hsü, *The North China Problem* (Shanghai, 1937), pp. 3–6; The Royal Institute of International Affairs, *China and Japan* (New York, 1938), p. 46; Quigley and Blakeslee, *op. cit.*, pp. 55–56.

[70] Shuhsi Hsü, *op. cit.*, pp. 6–10.

[71] *Ibid.*, pp. 10–15.

[72] George H. Blakeslee, *Conflicts of Policy in the Far East* (New York, 1934), pp. 22–24; Hsü, *op. cit.*, pp. 61–73.

[73] Shuhsi Hsü, *How the Far Eastern War Was Begun* (Shanghai, 1938), pp. 37–42.

[74] Shuhsi Hsü, *The North China Problem*, pp. 30–33.   [75] *Ibid.*, pp. 34–35.

Mah: Japan 113

Inner Mongolia;[76] the emergence of a semi-independent government for the provinces of Hopeh and Chahar in December, 1935;[77] the invasion and occupation of northern Chahar in December, 1935;[78] the insistence upon "joint defense against Communism" as a pretext for moving and stationing Japanese troops in China, particularly in Inner Mongolia; Hirota's "Three Principles" of January, 1936;[79] and the invasion of Suiyüan in November, 1936,[80] up to the "Lukouchiao Incident" of July 7, 1937[81]—all these are but a brief chronological summary of some of the military and political weapons of war which were hurled at China in time of peace.

When Manchuria was first invaded, China appealed to the League of Nations, but to no avail.[82] Nonetheless, in her knowledge that war would work untold disaster on millions of her innocent noncombatants and retard the progress of the urgent work of national reconstruction, China continued to be guided by the chief aim of endeavoring to preserve peace at all costs. She met warlike acts with passive resistance, and to this end suffered humiliation after humiliation; but Japan was insatiable. To appease the enemy, Chinese concessions which involved the restoration of normal trade relations, rail communication, and postal service with Japanese-occupied

---

[76] *Ibid.*, p. 35.
[77] *Ibid.*, p. 34.
[78] *Ibid.*, p. 35.
[79] Albert T. Lu, *Hirota's Three Principles vis-à-vis China*, Council of International affairs, Nanking, Vol. 1, No. 7; Bisson, *op. cit.*, pp. 124–127; Quigley and Blakeslee, *op. cit.*, pp. 93–94.
[80] Bisson, *op. cit.*, pp. 148–149.
[81] *Ibid.*, pp. 8–15.
[82] Henry L. Stimson, *The Far Eastern Crisis* (New York, 1936).

The Renaissance of Asia

Manchuria, the leasing of land and residences for the use of Japanese military forces stationed in eastern Hopeh in violation of the "demilitarized zone," and the establishment of air communication with the area under Japanese military occupation, including Jehol, north of the Great Wall, verged upon the *de facto* recognition of the Japanese-sponsored puppet regime created in Manchuria and Jehol.[88] In Hopeh Province, China had also withdrawn Chinese forces that were considered unfriendly toward Japan, and had dismissed from their posts high officials, including the governor, who were listed by Japan as *personae non gratae,* and replaced them with virtual Japanese appointees. And to further satisfy Japan's demands, all Chinese patriotic organizations and activities which Japan denounced as being "anti-Japanese" in complexion and spirit were officially or unofficially dissolved, or at least suppressed and hushed. By such drastic measures, among others, adopted to placate the enemy on the one hand and to neutralize, if possible, military pressure on the other, Chinese authority was gravely compromised and Chinese patriotism strained to the bursting point.

China bowed and bent before military might, but the sum of all efforts at conciliation and surrender was absolute futility. Even while China was giving way to Japanese military pressure and political demands, Japan did not desist from further invading Chinese territory in Chahar Province north of Hopeh. Moreover, in the closing months of 1935, when Japan was frustrated in her attempt to detach the five northern provinces from China, she arbitrarily seized the so-called

---

[88] Shuhsi Hsü, *The North China Problem*, pp. 10–15.

Mah: Japan 115

"demilitarized zone" and turned it into an active base of operations in pursuance of two objectives: one, to strike a paralyzing blow at China's economic and financial stability; the other, to separate at least two of the five provinces of North China—Hopeh and Chahar—and to include them within Japan's expanding political sphere of influence. In the execution of the first objective, mass smuggling operations by Japanese and Koreans of enormous quantities of Japanese goods into China were carried out, with the open connivance and under the protection of Japanese military, diplomatic, and consular authorities in North China. This wholesale illicit dumping into China through eastern Hopeh of Japanese goods valued at hundreds of millions of dollars, without payment of a single duty, severely undermined the revenue of the Chinese national government.[84] On the other hand, vast quantities of Chinese silver, a prohibited article of export at the time, were moved out of China by Japanese smugglers in similar fashion.[85]

In furtherance of the second objective, Japan's North China garrison, with headquarters at Tientsin, was forthwith strengthened by the addition of several thousand more troops, following which Japanese military activities were intensified and its sphere of operations extended over an ever-widening area in Hopeh. Northern Chahar was invaded and occupied. The net result was the forced reorganization of Chahar and Hopeh provinces under a semi-independent government—

---

[84] Albert T. Lu, *The Unabated Smuggling Situation in North China*, Council of International Affairs, Nanking, Vol. I, No. 11; Bisson, *op. cit.*, pp. 129–134; Quigley and Blakeslee, *op. cit.*, pp. 87–88.

[85] Bisson, *op. cit.*, p. 129.

the Hopeh-Chahar Political Council—and the appointment to this new governing body of a corps of Japanese "advisers" to "guide" its destiny.

Yet Japanese attacks did not stop here. From their newly established base in eastern Hopeh—whence Japanese political, military, and economic pressure was increasingly exerted upon local and central Chinese authorities—there appeared an army of Japanese narcotic peddlers, an invariable part of Japanese activities in China, who brazenly carried on their iniquitous traffic in Hopeh under the very nose of the Chinese authorities. Within the base itself these Japanese "traders" were also engaged in establishing, without official interference, gambling dens, houses of prostitution, and pawnshops without number. Elsewhere in China, Japanese spies and agents by the thousands were defiantly performing their nefarious assignments under various guises.

Such being the irreconcilable state of affairs since September 18, 1931, with no sign appearing on the horizon of any abatement in Japanese aggression, China decided that the limit of endurance had been reached. On July 7, 1937, when Japan fired the spark of open armed conflict at Lukouchiao, and peremptorily demanded control of five Chinese provinces in North China, aggregating some 400,000 square miles of productive territory and inhabited by more than 80,000,000 people,[86] China sounded the clarion call for the supreme sacrifice of the land in defense of an ancient birthright.

Japan's war of aggression is a ruthless campaign of conquest. To achieve her aims of becoming the unquestioned

---

[86] *The China Year Book*, 1935, pp. 2–4.

Mah: Japan 117

mistress of Eastern Asia, she stoops low. Her warfare is brutal.[87] Innocent noncombatants, men, women, and children alike, are slaughtered without mercy. Her systematic destruction of cultural institutions, of universities and colleges, of libraries, and of all schools accessible to her military, naval, or air forces, reveals a policy that is dangerous to world order and progress. Brute force and the law of the jungle guide her behavior, and no treaties are sacred nor pledges binding. She defies without compunction the standards of international law and order; by her invasion of China she has violated the Covenant of the League of Nations, the Pact of Paris, and the Nine-Power Treaty; and it is not to be forgotten that in 1933 she denounced the Washington Naval Treaty because it was not in consonance with her own aspirations for naval dominance in the Pacific.

Like a Colossus drunk with power, Japan stands astride a vast continent and thirsts for land and sea. Her actions bespeak the wild desires of an unholy mission of world conquest, but her spokesmen declare to the world that it is only Japan's "immutable policy" of establishing a "new order in East Asia."[88] Likewise her so-called peace terms are insidious. "Coöperation" professes to be the watchword, but the pronouncement works on the assumption that China is already conquered and subjugated by Japan, and that Chinese territory is already Japanese territory. Like the "peace terms" offered to China on December 22, 1938,[89] therefore, which are intelligible only by reading between the lines, the various

---
[87] H. J. Timperley, *Japanese Terror in China* (New York, 1938).
[88] *Japan Times*, November 3, 1938.
[89] *New York Times*, December 22, 1938.

118   *The Renaissance of Asia*

enunciations of the Japanese Government on the "new order" are equally ambiguous and typical of Japanese diplomatic quibbling. The "new order in East Asia" is simply the modern, 20th-century version of the old Hideyoshi dream enlarged substantially and dressed up in vague and euphemistic language, accompanied by a polite demand that the powers of the world had best take heed and accord it due recognition. It is but an artificial façade designed to camouflage ulterior designs of world domination. China is but a means to an end. Under the "new order," East Asia is to be Japan's private preserve, the Open Door is slammed, and Western interests and influence barred from China and the Far East. The "new order" proclaims a racial as well as a political war. As Mr. Henry L. Stimson aptly said in his statement before the Foreign Relations Committee of the Senate on April 6, 1939, the Japanese are the "militaristic enemies who by conquest are trying to turn China into a reservoir of potential future aggression against the rest of the world."[90] Verily, with East Asia in her palm, Japan is in a position to prevail over the whole of Asia; with Asia under her thumb, she can safely proceed to rule the Pacific; and with dominion over the Pacific, the way is open for her to wield a master hand in world affairs. Whether or not Eastern Siberia, French Indo-China, Siam, British Malaya, India, the Dutch East Indies, Australia, and the Philippine Islands may soon be brought into her political orbit, will be a contingency dependent upon the outcome of Japan's war of conquest in China.

---

[90] *New York Times*, April 6, 1939.

SOVIET RUSSIA IN ASIA

ROBERT J. KERNER
PROFESSOR OF MODERN EUROPEAN HISTORY
IN THE UNIVERSITY OF CALIFORNIA

Lecture delivered May 1, 1939

SOVIET RUSSIA IN ASIA

SIBERIA has been called a "second North America," a "world unborn," and a "land of promise."[1] To many Americans it has been a land of prisons, of terrible cold, and of vast, impenetrable forests—too far away and too little known to be of significance except when sables or exiles come into the conversation. Some of us sometimes even forget that Russia is in Asia and on the Pacific. And yet it appears all too likely that the region from the Urals to Lake Baikal will become the very axis of the future industrial development of the Soviet Union. All signs point to the conclusion that the Soviet Union is determined not only to defend its position in Asia, but to play an important role in the destinies of that continent and the Pacific as well.

The conquest of Siberia, which began in 1581, started as a raid by the pirate Yermak, to scatter the natives beyond the Urals—who in turn had raided the Russians from time to time—and to get furs and silver. It ended for landlocked Russia on the shores of the Pacific in 1639. The actual acquisition of Siberia was carried out not by the policy of raids, but by

[1] For bibliography see Robert J. Kerner, *Northeastern Asia: A Selected Bibliography* (Berkeley, University of California Press), 2 vols. For general reading, among others see N. V. Kiuner, *Lekstii po istorii i geografii Sibiri* (Vladivostok, 1919); Maurice Courant, *La Sibérie colonie russe jusqu'à la construction du Transsibérien* (Paris, 1920); *Aziatskaia Rossiia* (St. Petersburg, 1914, 3 vols.); Vladimir (Z. Volpicelli), *Russia and the Pacific and the Siberian Railway* (London, 1899); Leo Pasvolsky, *Russia in the Far East* (London, 1922); Victor A. Yakhontoff, *Russia and the Soviet Union in the Far East* (New York, 1931); A. Lobanov-Rostovsky, *Russia and Asia* (New York, 1933); and N. N. Baranskii, *Ekonomicheskaia geografiia S.S.S.R.* (Moscow, 1935).

The Renaissance of Asia

a process, old among Russians, of dominating the successive river basins and the portages between the rivers. Its motive power was tribute and trade in furs.[2] It was one result of the historic urge of the Russians to reach the sea. Today Siberia, or more properly the Far Eastern region, represents to Russians one of their fundamental historical yearnings. To be cut off from the Pacific would strike deeply into Russian consciousness, and no sacrifice to retain this access to the sea would be considered too great. This is one of the factors in the background of recent developments. The possible loss of the Ukraine and the precarious Baltic coast line bring to Russians the same feelings as does contemplation of the Far Eastern region. The loss of access to the sea would mean the loss of Russia's independence. The Russian nation paid dearly in the past for this access to the sea in the highly centralized and despotic government of the Tsars.[3]

For over three centuries Siberia and Central Asia (attached only toward the end of the period) were colonies and, as such, were exploited. The former for two centuries brought in a rich harvest of furs as well as a lucrative trade in Chinese tea, while serving as a penal settlement for Russia's rebels and bad men. Later, gold was obtained. Central Asia was sought for its gold and wool and its transit trade and as a protecting flank for Siberia. Later on, cotton culture was developed. Cen-

---

[2] See the forthcoming publication of the author, *The Urge to the Sea: The Course of Russian History—The Rôle of Rivers, Portages, Ostrogs, Monasteries, and Furs* (now ready for the press).

[3] See Robert J. Kerner, "The Foreign Policies of Russia," in *The Foreign Policies of the Great Powers* (Berkeley, University of California Press, 1939); V. Motylev, *Zarozhdenie i razvitie tikhookeanskogo uzla protivorechii* (Moscow, 1939).

tral Asia also had a strategic "nuisance value" at the gates of British India. The natives, eventually outnumbered by Russians in Siberia, but always overwhelmingly outnumbering the Russians in Central Asia, were exposed to a process of Russification. Moreover, Russian administration in Asia was ordinarily corrupt and brutal. Under such conditions no rational and intelligent development could be expected. And none took place.

Then came the Russo-Turkish war, which, though victorious for Russia on the battlefield, ended in a defeat at the Congress of Berlin in 1878 at the hands of England and Austria. The unification of Bulgaria in 1885, and the elevation of Prince Ferdinand of Coburg to the princely throne of that country in 1887, presented Russia with the alternative of intervention and another war, this time with Austria and England, or of a retreat. The Kuldja dispute roused up China. The treaty of 1885 between Japan and China in regard to Korea confronted Russia at the other extremity of her far-flung empire with a new and aggressive neighbor. It was under such circumstances that the Balkans were "put on ice," as contemporary opinion had it, and an understanding with Austria in regard to the political status quo in that region arranged, which held for nearly twenty years. The construction of the Transsiberian Railway was begun in 1891 chiefly because of its strategic significance.[4] This opened a new era for Siberia, the period of transition from a colony to an integral part of Russia which lasted for over four decades. It was the begin-

---

[4] A. N. Kulomzin, S. V. Sabler, and I. V. Sosnovskii, *Sibirskaia zheleznaia doroga* (St. Petersburg, 1903), p. 72.

The Renaissance of Asia

ning of the renaissance in Russian Asia. It also initiated a new development in the foreign policy of Russia, a period of mysterious adventure in Asia and the Far East which ended in defeat in the Russo-Japanese war.

The building of the Transsiberian was notice, especially to Japan, that Russia would defend her position in Asia. As is well known, Japan answered in 1894 by the Sino-Japanese War, in which Korea came under Japanese domination. Japan was forced by the intervention of Russia, Germany, and France to relinquish her territorial acquisition in the Liaotung peninsula in return for an increased indemnity, while Russia by the secret Sino-Russian treaty of May, 1896, embarked on the venture of building the Chinese Eastern and other Manchurian railways, as well as of utilizing the ice-free naval base of Port Arthur and the commercial port of Dalny (now called Dairen). At the same time a nebulous project of dominating China by acquiring preponderance in its Mongolian and Tibetan hinterland was begun under the inspiration of the Buriat Tibetan doctor Badmaiev. Some such idea as that the Tsar should be the political protector of the Buddhist Church through an arrangement with the Tibetan Dalai Lama was a part of this scheme. Other adventurers involved the imperial family in timber and gold-mining concessions in Korea, Manchuria, and Mongolia, while Witte himself seems to have dreamed at one time of a vast Russo-Chinese empire.[5] All these dreams crashed in the Russo-

---
[5] P. A. Badmaiev, *Rossiia i Kitai* (St. Petersburg, 1905); V. P. Semennikov, *Za kulisami tsarisma* (Leningrad, 1925); B. A. Romanov, *Rossiia v Manzhurii* (Leningrad, 1928); A. Ular (pseud.), *A Russo-Chinese Empire* (Westminster, 1904).

Japanese War. The Treaty of Portsmouth, by which Russia lost her railroads and concessions in southern Manchuria, as well as her territory in the southern half of the island of Sakhalin, became the starting point not of a cycle of revenge, but of an increasingly intimate alliance after 1907 by which Japan annexed Korea, Russia obtained preponderance in Outer Mongolia, and between them Inner Mongolia and Manchuria were divided into spheres of influence.[6] In the same way England advanced to a special position in Tibet. This period ended in the Bolshevik revolution of November, 1917.

On the other hand, the building of the Transsiberian Railway for the first time brought hundreds of thousands of settlers into Siberia. The railroad was completed as a single-track trunk line in 1903. In 1897 the population of Siberia (excepting Kamchatka and Sakhalin) was 8,184,400. In 1917 the same area had a population of 14,455,300, an increase of more than 6,000,000 in 20 years, or 76 per cent. By 1914 western Siberia had little or no free land (without great previous preparation) for settlement. In 1915 it was estimated that Siberia could absorb safely only about 200,000 settlers a year. The cities of Siberia grew faster than the countryside. Siberia itself was increasing over two and a half times faster in population than European Russia. By 1917, 80 per cent of her population was Russian.[7] All this led to economic and cultural activity

[6] Ernest B. Price, *The Russo-Japanese Treaties of 1907–1916 concerning Manchuria and Mongolia* (Baltimore, 1933).

[7] Anatole V. Baikalov, "The Conquest and Colonization of Siberia since 1894," *Slavonic Review*, Vol. 10, No. 30 (April, 1932), pp. 557–571, and Vol. 11, No. 32 (January, 1933), pp. 328–340.

which was interrupted by the World War and the Revolution, and by the intervention which followed and lasted here until 1922.

In November, 1917, the Bolsheviks seized power in Russia. They appealed at once for an immediate general peace. They had as their objectives the Communization of Russia and a world revolution to create a union of soviet socialist republics as the outcome of the World War. In contrast with Russia under the Tsars, with its trilogy of Russian autocracy, Russian orthodoxy, and Russian nationalism—a sort of religious political imperialism,—the Bolsheviks had as their objective a world-wide federation of Communist nations, a sort of mystical social imperialism.

Just as the Russo-Japanese War and the Russian revolution in 1905 tremendously affected Asia, so now the Bolshevik revolution in 1917 and the subsequent reaction which has crystalized in the Anti-Comintern Pact after 1936 are the cause of decisive events, not only in Asia, but on a grander scale in the world at large. The conjuncture of events in 1905 led to Japan's leadership in the Far East and to revolution in China, to reform in Siam, and to the awakening of Hindu India. The Russian revolution of 1905 gave an example for revolution to Persia in 1906, to Turkey in 1908, and to unrest in Moslem India which soon coalesced into the Indian National Movement. It also startled the many nations and races in the Russian Empire from their lethargy. And now the Bolshevik revolution, both by example and by active propaganda, inspired revolution in Turkey, Persia, Afghanistan, Tibet, Chinese Turkestan, Mongolia, and China proper, in addition to further unrest in India. The reaction, led by Japan since 1931, now embraces Germany and Italy and those states which have joined the Anti-Comintern Pact since 1936.

The Bolshevik leaders, some of them against their better judgment, were led to carry out at once a complete revolution in Russia, now known as military Communism, which failed in the famine of 1921. In the midst of civil war and intervention, Lenin[8] had founded the Third International in 1919 with the hope that the impetus created by the World War toward revolution might be organized through Communist parties everywhere into a world revolution. From the very beginning in 1917 it was the faith of the Bolsheviks that the World War would result in revolution everywhere, and Europe was their chief hope. Many of them despaired of making backward Russia a Communist state unless more advanced industrialized states, like Germany, England, and the United States, were revolutionized under Communist leadership. In fact, some of them believed that the Russian revolution could not be saved except in that way. In this hope the Bolsheviks were bitterly disappointed, chiefly because to

[8] See Michael T. Florinsky, *World Revolution and the U.S.S.R.* (New York, Macmillan, 1933), pp. 145 ff.; C. L. James, *World Revolution, 1917-1936: The Rise and Fall of the Communist International* (New York, Pioneer Publishers, 1937), 429 pp.; Leon Trotsky, *The Third International after Lenin* (New York, Pioneer Publishers, 1936), 357 pp.; his *The Revolution Betrayed* (New York, Doubleday, 1937), 308 pp.; and *The Case of Leon Trotsky . . .* by the Preliminary Commission of Inquiry (New York, Harper, 1937), 617 pp. Further material may be found in Arthur Rosenberg, *History of Bolshevism from Marx to the First Five-Year Plan* (London, Oxford University Press, 1934), 280 pp.; in *Communist International* (Leningrad-Moscow, 1919–); and in Stalin's "Answer to Comrade Ivan Filippovich Ivanov," *Pravda*, February 14, 1938.

Europeans Bolshevik methods and plans appeared too crude. These dreams were liquidated in Europe by 1923, the effort to Bolshevize Germany having failed.

Lenin, among the first to sense this development in Europe, proposed in the Second Congress of the Third International in 1920 to revolutionize Asia and thus weaken capitalism in the European powers through the loss of their colonies and imperialistic advantages in Asia. A conference of Asiatic nations was called that year at Baku to promote the program.[*] It should be noted, however, that if it was a mistake to try immediately to transform Russia, a backward country, into a Communist state, it was a greater mistake to try to transform into Communist states countries in Asia still more backward and more conservative than Russia. This effort failed and was liquidated in the Chinese national revolution in 1927, as well as in other Asiatic countries before that time.

In this first decade of Soviet rule in Russia (1917–1927) we note, then, that the chief emphasis was on foreign policy with the objective of revolution outside of Russia. Within that country there is the record of the failure to communize Russia by 1921 and the adoption of the compromise New Economic Policy. Asiatic Russia was not completely under Soviet rule until 1922 and hence was relatively neglected. The emphasis on revolution in Asia after the Conference of Baku in 1920 was accompanied on the Russian side with the giving up of imperialistic privileges and concessions of the old Russia and by cultural autonomy and federation inside the Soviet

---

[*] Louis Fischer, *The Soviets in World Affairs* (New York, 1930), Vol. 1, pp. 283, 385.

Union. This had a great attraction for the Asiatic peoples ruled by Europeans and just beginning to sense the stirring emotions of nationalism. In so many words, European domination was lifting—Soviet Russia was the first to offer liberation. They sought to take advantage of independence and equality for themselves, but, as will be seen, for the most part they balked at the export to them of Bolshevism as soon as they recovered from their surprise at the renunciation of Tsarist privileges and power. This development may be illustrated in Soviet relations with Turkey, Persia, Afghanistan, and China during this period of the first decade.

Soviet Russia denounced the secret treaties in regard to the acquisition of the Straits and Armenia. The domination of the Straits by the British after the armistice and the National Turkish Revolution under the leadership of Mustapha Kemal Pasha led Bolshevik leaders to support the latter and to sign a treaty recognizing Nationalist Turkey on March 16, 1921. Soviet Russia received Batum; Turkey retained Kars and Ardahan. The Bolsheviks proposed a conference of the Black Sea states to regulate the question of the Straits. While Turkey obtained her independence at the Conference of Lausanne in 1923, the Straits were disarmed and neutralized, and passage of warships was permitted under certain conditions, an arrangement which Soviet Russia hotly contested as it opened her to an attack by sea. Turkey, however, did not adopt the soviet system; even though she has since signed a series of treaties with Soviet Russia, which indicates very close relations. The revision at the Conference of Montreux in 1936 of the provisions of the Treaty of Lausanne in regard to the

Straits has measurably improved Soviet Russia's position on the Black Sea.[10] Turkey has accepted economic assistance, not only from the Bolsheviks, but from Germany and England as well. Her chief desire is to remain independent. She controls the strategic key to the economic life of Soviet Russia and it is to the latter's interest to maintain Turkey's independence, even though Turkey will not tolerate Communism on her territory. Thus Soviet-Turkish relations have led not to another Communist state, but to a national bourgeois regime of a fascist character.

British domination of Persia in the last days of the war led to the signature of an agreement in 1919 which virtually established a British protectorate in which the Anglo-Persian Oil Company played a prominent role. Two years later, after the confusion which followed the triumph of the Bolshevik army over that of General Denikin in southern Russia, Soviet Russia signed the Treaty of Moscow, February 26, 1921, which liquidated the British hold on Persia and called for an alliance against encroachment by a third power. The Bolshevik domination of northern and central Persia was, in turn, ended by the bourgeois national revolution in 1925 headed by Riza Khan, who assumed the title of Shah. Here another adventure was terminated in favor of a fascist regime.

At first it seemed that the most important success would be recorded in Afghanistan when Amanullah Khan succeeded in rebelling against the British protectorate and gained com-

---

[10] Harry N. Howard, *The Partition of Turkey* (Norman, Oklahoma, 1931), pp. 285–297, and "The Straits after the Montreux Conference," *Foreign Affairs*, Vol. 15, No. 1 (October, 1936), pp. 199–202.

plete independence. He naturally turned to Russia because of his desire rapidly to modernize Afghanistan, and signed a treaty at Moscow on February 28, 1921, in which Russia gained such advantages as to create a preponderance. A bourgeois national reaction developed and drove Amanullah into exile in 1929, thus ending Soviet preponderance. A fascist type of independent state was established.

The same process with some modifications was repeated in Russian relations with China. In 1919 and 1920 Russia renounced her concessions and special privileges. Some of the remnants of the anti-Bolshevik Siberian forces appeared in Mongolia under Baron Ungern von Sternberg, who dreamed of a Mongol empire after the manner of Genghis Khan. Such an empire would have cut across Siberia to include the Mongol Buriats in the Baikal region, if it had been successful. He was defeated by the Bolsheviks at Troitskosavsk in August, 1921. The Bolsheviks thereafter overran Mongolia and signed a treaty of friendship with Mongolia that year. This led within three years to the establishment of Soviet Outer Mongolia, in which many, but not all, the features of the Soviet system were adopted.[21] This is also true of the Uriankhai district which seceded from Mongolia and under the Tannu Tuva People's Republic became a part of the Soviet orbit. To all appearances Soviet protectorates were established here and have remained so to this day, the only results of the strenuous attempt at world revolution.

In the meanwhile, China had protested the Soviet encroachment on Mongolia. The reëstablishment in 1922 of Soviet rule

---
[21] Fischer, *op. cit.*, Vol. 2, pp. 531-539, 543, 635, 727, 826 ff.

The Renaissance of Asia

in the Far Eastern Province and the desire of Russia to regain control of the Chinese Eastern Railway, operated until then by White Russians under Inter-Allied control, led to decisive negotiations with the Chinese government in 1924. By the treaty of May 31, China recognized the Soviet Union and the Soviet Union recognized the sovereignty of China in Outer Mongolia. The Chinese Eastern Railway was declared to be the joint commercial enterprise of both, with the right of purchase vested in China under stipulated conditions. Later that year a similar agreement was made with Chang Tso-lin, the war lord of Manchuria.

In the meanwhile, in 1923 the Third International had supplied the Cantonese Kuomintang, under Sun Yat-sen, with an organizer named Michael Borodin and a military staff. It began the training of a revolutionary army and a party administrative force. In the next three years it swept everything before it and developed the able and resolute leadership of Chiang Kai-shek, who, after the capture of Hankow and Nanking and the domination of central China, broke with the Bolsheviks in December, 1927, and forced them to withdraw across the Gobi Desert. A raid on the Soviet embassy in Peking in April had disclosed ample evidence of Communist activity. Stalin himself explained this situation in a discussion on "The Revolution in China and the Tasks of the Communist International":

> Nanking and the Nanking government represent the center of the national counterrevolution. The policy of support to the Hankow government is at the same time the policy of the development of the bourgeois democratic revolution with all the consequences resulting therefrom. From this follows the participation

of Communists in the Hankow Kuomintang and the Hankow revolutionary government, a participation which does not exclude but presupposes incessant criticism by the Communists of the halfway measures and vacillations of their allies in the Kuomintang. This participation of the Communists should be utilized for the purpose of making the role of hegemony in the Chinese bourgeois democratic revolution easier for the proletariat and bringing nearer the moment of transition to the proletarian revolution. For the moment the bourgeois democratic revolution moves onwards to the transition to the proletarian revolution—we must create Soviets of workers', peasants' and soldiers' deputies, as factors of dyarchy, as organs of the struggle for the new power, as organs of the new power, the power of the Soviets. Then the Communist Alliance inside the Kuomintang must be replaced by a Communist alliance outside, and the Communist Party must become the only leader of the new revolution in China. To propose now, as Comrades Trotsky and Zinoviev do, the immediate formation of Soviets of workers' and peasants' deputies, and the immediate creation of a dyarchy—now, when the bourgeois democratic revolution is still in the early stages of its development, when the Kuomintang is the most suitable form of organization for the national-democratic revolution in China—this would mean to disorganize the revolutionary movement, to weaken the Hankow government, to facilitate its fall and to help Chang Tso-lin and Chiang Kai-shek.[13]

In this one glimpses the policy of the man who that year triumphed over Trotsky; and this triumph produced a change in the fundamental policy of the Third International as practiced for eight years since its creation. Here is the best statement from Stalin of the policy of the "united front." A new period in the history of the Soviet Union was ushered in.

---
[13] *Communist International*, Vol. 4, No. 10 (June 30, 1927), pp. 200–207.

The policy of violent and immediate world revolution of the Third International had ended in failure in Europe in 1923 and in Asia in 1927. Soviet Outer Mongolia and Tannu Tuva were its only tangible results.

The Stalin-Trotsky controversy was more than a personal conflict; it was a struggle to determine the fundamental policies of the Soviet Union and the Third International.[13]

Trotsky believed in the theory of permanent revolution. He came to the view that the New Economic Policy inaugurated in 1921 would make Russia a capitalist country—in other words, the Bolshevik revolution would fail and the leaders lose their grip on that country—unless a violent and immediate world revolution, engineered by the Third International with all the resources of Russia behind it, succeeded. He would exploit the peasants of Russia for such a purpose in order to save the revolution in Russia.

Stalin argued that socialism could be built in a single country. He stated then, and has since confirmed the statement, that socialism could not triumph completely in Soviet Russia unless other important countries ultimately became socialistic. This was the significance of the policy of the united front, already explained by him as in the quotation above. He believed that a continuation of violent and aggressive activity on the part of the Third International and singlehanded activity on the part of Communists in national revolutions would lead to the intervention of capitalist powers in the Soviet Union.

When he triumphed over Trotsky in 1927-28, he charted

---
[13] See note 8, above.

the course of his country along lines of peace—he put the Soviet Union on the defensive, he set it to work on the five-year plans, and he transformed the Third International into a supplementary defense of the Soviet Union with long-range instead of immediate objectives. These, in the main, have been the fundamentals of Stalin's policy ever since he won power.

This of course brought about an entirely different orientation in Soviet internal policy. The New Economic Policy had succeeded so well that the prewar level of production in industry and agriculture was in sight in 1927-28. In fact, it had succeeded too well and there were increasing fears that Soviet Russia would become capitalist in form of society.

There followed the adoption of three five-year plans. The first ended in 1932, the second in 1937, and the third is scheduled to end in 1942.[14]

The First Five-Year Plan was centered on the creation of a heavy industry capable of providing the Societ Union with the sinews of war in the event of intervention by a coalition of capitalist states. During this period the first extensive coal, iron, and electrical energy base in the Ukraine, known as the Donbas-Dnieprostroi, was launched. The plan was hardly on its way before it was discovered that this European base would not be sufficient for the Soviet Union as a whole. There was also the possibility of the loss of the Ukraine. Events in

[14] *Piatiletnii plan* (Moscow, 1930, 3 vols.); G. T. Grinko, *The Five-Year Plan of the Soviet Union* (New York, 1930); *Vtoroi piatiletnii plan razvitiia narodnogo khoziaistva S.S.S.R. (1933-1937)* (Moscow, 1934), in English translation, *The Second Five-Year Plan* (New York, International Publishers, n.d.); for the Third Five-Year Plan, see *Industriia*, March 16-21, 1939.

136   *The Renaissance of Asia*

the Far East were already in the making which were to lead to the Japanese seizure of Manchuria in 1931. It was under such circumstances that the First All-Union Conference on the Distribution of Productive Forces[15] was called, that year. Of the eight regions recommended as possible extensive industrial bases, six were in Asia: the Urals, Central Asia, Ural-Irtysh, Kuznetsk-Minusinsk, Baikal, and the Transcaucasus. This recommendation was a result of geological surveys and engineering investigations. Thus the slogan "Shift industry to the east" gained concrete form.

In 1931, therefore, the construction of the second coal and metal base of the Soviet Union, known as the Ural-Kuznetsk or the Ural-Kuzbas Combine, was begun. The abundant iron of Magnitogorsk was shipped eastward to the rich coal reserves of Kuznetsk and the coal of Kuznetsk to the iron of Magnitogorsk. This base was developed during the Second Five-Year Plan, with numerous other industries dependent on it. It was stated in 1934 that "the Ural-Kuzbas mined one-fifth of the total quantity of coal produced in the U.S.S.R. and 30 per cent of the total quantity of ore extracted, smelted over a quarter of the total quantity of pig iron, put out one-sixth of the total quantity of coke and almost a quarter of the total output of the chemical industry of the U.S.S.R."[16]

[15] Bruce Hopper, "Eastward the Course of Soviet Empire," *Foreign Affairs*, Vol. 14, No. 1 (October, 1935), pp. 37–50; *Trudy pervoi vsesoiuznoi konferentsii po razmeshcheniiu proizvoditelnykh sil soiuza* (Moscow, 1931, 16 vols.).

[16] *Socialism Victorious* (London, Martin Lawrence, Ltd., n.d.), p. 628; *Problemy Uralo-Kuzbasskogo kombinata*, Vol. 2 (Leningrad, Akademiia Nauk, 1933). In 1938 Kuzbas produced 16,800,000 tons of coal, and Magnitogorsk 1,158,000 tons of pig iron.—*Industriia*, March 5, 18, 1939.

Kerner: Russia 137

After the beginning of the Second Five-Year Plan a third industrial base, farther east, was projected in concrete form and is being constructed under the Third Five-Year Plan. It is known as the Angaro-Yenisei or the Angarastroi, and is situated around the extensive water-power resources of the Angara tributary of the Yenisei River.[17] It was estimated that electric power to the magnitude of 115 billion kilowatt hours could be developed here. This is to be taken in connection with estimated reserves of iron amounting to 500 million tons in eastern Siberia. Angarastroi is designed as the base for the region of Lake Baikal and the Far East. In view of the results obtained by these investigations, it seemed most likely that the future industrial core of the Soviet Union would shift from European Russia to the Asiatic region from the Urals to Lake Baikal. Taken together with Central Asia, the eastern regions were found to have 80.5 per cent of the energy resources (coal, shale, oil, turf, gas, wood, and water power) of the Soviet Union, 28 to 40 per cent of the iron, 87 to 97 per cent of the copper, 95 per cent of the zinc, 96 per cent of the rare metals, 60 per cent of the area suitable for wheat, and 72 per cent of the yearly growth of forest.[18]

The development of navigation in the Arctic and the economic revival of northern Siberia were undertaken with great energy during the Second Five-Year Plan. The *Sibiriakov* made the first "real northwest passage" in the summer of 1932 from Arkhangelsk in European Russia to Vladivostok.

---
[17] *Angaro-Eniseiskaia problema. Trudy pervoi vsesoiuznoi konferentsii po razmeshcheniiu proizvoditelnykh sil soiuza*, Vol. 16, pp. 229–238.

[18] *Trudy pervoi vsesoiuznoi konferentsii*, Vol. 16, pp. 45–51.

In 1936, under unfavorable conditions, fourteen through voyages were made and 156 ships traveled the Arctic seas. Along the northern sea route—significant as an alternative strategic road to reach the Far East if other avenues should be closed—radio and weather stations, air bases, and thriving towns are springing up. Igarka, on the Yenisei, is a center for a new timber and wheat development.[19]

The cotton, wool, and copper of central Asia are taken care of on the ground by textile and smelting industries. Tanneries, shoe factories, and packing plants have been built in the ranges of Kazakistan.

This industrial development is dependent upon railway and river communications, which are being extended more rapidly per mile in Asia than in Europe. Besides the Turk-Sib Railway which joins central Asia with Siberia and skirts close enough to the Chinese frontier to drain Chinese Turkestan and northwestern Mongolia, there are the Baikal-Amur and the Lena River lines now being built, which will feed into the Angarastroi. In addition, the Transsiberian has been double tracked and a second northern grand trunk line extending across the length of Siberia has been projected.

From this cursory survey we may conclude, after discounting a good deal of exaggeration, that the Soviet Union is determined to defend its position in Asia and on the Pacific. Siberia and central Asia are no longer colonies, but vital parts of the state. The Soviet Union is an important factor in the renaissance of Asia. Premier Molotov said recently, "We re-

---

[19] T. A. Taracouzio, *Soviets in the Arctic* (New York, 1938), pp. 141–251, esp. pp. 244–245.

gard the Far East as a mighty outpost of Soviet power in the East which requires further strengthening by all means available."[20] Success in this regard is calculated by the leader in the Kremlin as powerful propaganda by example in Asia. Will Japan strike before the Ural-Baikal industrial development is finished?

If we examine the foreign policy of the period since the triumph of Stalin over Trotsky in 1927-28, we note that it was stressed officially as one of peace and coexistence with capitalist states and characterized by numerous nonaggression and neutrality treaties the purpose of which was to defend the Soviet Union from attack during the period of transition from an agricultural to an industrial state. Perhaps nothing done inside so shook the foundations of Russia as the brusk policy of collectivization of the peasants. It was in the midst of this situation that Japan advanced into Manchuria and occupied even the northern sector and forced the relinquishment by sale of the Chinese Eastern Railway in 1935. Japan's new position in Manchuria and eastern Inner Mongolia weakened strategically the position of the Soviet Union in eastern Siberia and exposed to interruption the only railroad line to Vladivostok. It necessitated the building of the Baikal-Amur Railway and of Soviet Harbor; and further Japanese advance into Inner Mongolia was to be resisted by the Soviet Union. It also increased the preponderant activity of the latter in Chinese Turkestan.

The accession of Hitler to power in 1933 led to the end of

---
[20] Speech at the 18th Congress of the All-Union Communist Party. *Industriia*, March 16, 1939, p. 3.

the German-Russian entente which was created in 1922 at Rapallo, and to the entry of Soviet Russia into the League of Nations in 1934, as well as to the making of the Franco-Soviet and Czechoslovak-Soviet Pacts in 1935. The policy of the united front was adopted by the Seventh Congress of the Third International in that year. When, however, Germany and Japan signed the Anti-Comintern Pact on November 25, 1936, an entirely new situation was created, especially in the Far East. It seems certain that Russia's preoccupation with her industrialization precluded an active policy abroad, and her first reaction then was still to hope—as perhaps she still hopes—for some measure of accommodation with both Japan and Germany. If such a hope was entertained in the Kremlin, it has thus far been a mistaken one. A year later Italy adhered to the Pact and since then Manchukuo, Hungary, and Spain have publicly announced their adherence. In many ways the menacing declarations of the Third International played directly into the hands of the Anti-Comintern powers.

If we are to believe Hitler, Konoye, and Mussolini, as well as the men closest to them, and the recent Soviet revelations on the subject, the published Anti-Comintern Pact conceals an agreement to redistribute territories and sources of raw materials on a world-wide scale and to create a Fascist league of nations by a close coördination of aggressive moves in various parts of the world.[21] It is directed not only against the Soviet Union, using the Third International as a screen, but

---

[21] See Baron Iwakusu Ida, "The Meaning of the Japanese-German Pact," *Contemporary Japan*, March, 1937; *Völkerbund*, Vol. 7, No. 4, p. 64; W. H. Chamberlin, "The Rome-Berlin-Tokyo Axis," *Contemporary Japan*, June, 1938; and *Contemporary Manchuria*, March, 1938, pp. 79-89.

against France, England, and other countries as well. If the Soviet Union continues to dominate, with a tolerably intelligent and able leadership, the vast region which it now controls, Germany cannot hope to dominate Europe and Japan cannot be paramount in Asia and on the Pacific.

That the Third International and Communism are used as a screen by Japan is to be seen from the fact that from 1927 to the Sian incident in December, 1936, Chiang Kai-shek fought campaign after campaign against the Chinese Communists and succeeded in driving them across China to the northwest, all the while incurring the opposition of the Japanese. If Communism were not a screen for the Japanese conquest of China, Chiang Kai-shek would have been the best ally for Japan. As it was, Japanese encroachment in North China drove Chiang Kai-shek into the arms of the left wing of the Kuomintang and the Communists. What the Japanese did not want was a modernized, national, and independent bourgeois China. It would eventually have made their position in Manchuria, and possibly in Korea as well, untenable. It seems strange, but it is true, that the allies in this case, therefore, really should be Japan and the Soviet Union, since such a China is not at bottom desirable to the extremist leaders of either.

Recent events in Europe leading to the Munich accord and the virtual isolation of Soviet Russia further complicated that country's position. Sooner or later she must emerge from her isolation. She cannot remain isolated long. An opportunity of emergence appears to have been offered by the recent British reversal of policy. On the other hand, Japan has countered with the threat that she will sign a military alliance with Germany and Italy if the Soviet Union is included in the attempt to form a grand alliance against the Anti-Comintern powers in Europe.

Is British diplomacy once more on the brink of another Munich? Without Russia an effective alliance against Germany seems impossible. Is Soviet Russia reaping the harvest of the loud talk and ineffective work of the Third International, as well as of apparent internal difficulties shown in the purge? Can Germany, Italy, and Japan carry out their far-flung plans by revolution, intervention, and conquest, without incurring disaster? There seems to be a well-grounded and increasingly growing conviction that whatever America does or does not do will give the answer to these questions.

THE FUTURE OF CHINA

H. ARTHUR STEINER
ASSISTANT PROFESSOR OF POLITICAL SCIENCE
IN THE UNIVERSITY OF CALIFORNIA

Lecture delivered May 8, 1939

THE FUTURE OF CHINA

AN ADVENTURER into the realm of social prognostication quickly learns of the perils that beset his course. There are no dependable charts to guide him, and his goal must always remain an elusive mirage on the distant horizon. His expedition is discredited before it begins. But he undertakes it nevertheless—knowing that countless unpredictable variables enter into human and social affairs, and that he is himself an element in the scene he is to describe. Let him realize at the outset that the future is not abstractly detached from the past and present, however, and his effort may find its justification. Political prediction may fruitfully be utilized as a convenient device for appraising the broad tendencies of the present, for taking stock of the fundamental social current that is too often obscured by the fantastic whirling of its surface eddies.

We cannot escape the implications of China's tremendous proportions and of the highly fluid and dynamic condition in which she at present finds herself. Physical China has the dimensions of a subcontinent; her population is the world's largest; and of all living cultures hers is the oldest and the richest. Nowhere is there greater social ferment. If the harsher outlines are to be subtly shaded, her future must be painted on a canvas of suitable size. What is to be depicted is not an artificially personified political state, but a mass of humanity.

Between China and her future lies the present war with Japan. We must deal with that war as a fact, although our interest in it arises solely from the direct or indirect influences it may exert on the future of life in China. For the present we must neglect its social and political causes, its diplomatic preliminaries, its effects on the future of Japan, and its relation to the interplay of political forces in other parts of the world—aspects that are intrinsically important and would be vastly significant in another context.

China, engaged in a struggle for her very existence, has not alone to determine what her future will be like, but to question whether she will even have one of her own. There is no doubt in my mind that she will survive and that she faces a bright future. But for integral survival she must first master the most disastrous tendency of her recent history. China crossed the threshold of the 20th century into a future made uncertain by the loss of her suzerainty over the Maritime Provinces, Formosa, Annam, and Korea. Since 1900, she has lost the effective exercise of sovereignty in Tibet, Outer Mongolia, Sinkiang, and Manchuria. These losses evidenced the disruptive forces that were at work, but they did not until recently affect the basic situation in the Middle Kingdom. The present encroachments in China have a different character and are driving a wedge into the vital heart of China Proper. In twenty-two months of warfare Japan has destroyed effective Chinese sovereignty in an area of some 400,000 square miles, even though she has not very conclusively substituted her own. The Japanese invasion brings the historical tendency of partition to its crucial stage. China now fully appreciates that if she is to grasp and give conscious shape to her destiny she must first reverse that tendency by setting force against force. Her chances of expelling Japan from her territory must be appraised before her long future can be discussed.

Shortly after the fall of Canton and Hankow last October, the Japanese government announced the collapse of the citadels of Chinese resistance and branded the government of Chiang Kai-shek as "no longer anything but a local regime." That optimism was superficially justified. Japan held an impressive tactical advantage, controlling the ports that gave China her access by sea to the outside world, the lower Yangtze Valley, and the railway centers of the densely populated and wealthy Chinese plains. Possessed of the vital lines of communication by land and water, the Japanese armies for a while ceased their forward motion in the hope that the Chinese might share their conviction that the hostilities were at an end. What actually awaited them was the war in its second stage—now a war of rugged attrition where victory would rest with the side more adequately supplied with economic and financial sinews, better equipped for a wearing persistence of indefinite duration, and more doggedly determined to win.[1] These things the Japanese discovered when they re-

---

[1] Chiang Kai-shek proclaimed his plan of prolonged resistance on October 31, 1938 (*Jih pao* [Shanghai], November 1, 1938), and its details were confirmed after a staff meeting in Chungking, December 12 (*Sun huan jih pao* [Hongkong], December 14, 1938). Evidence of the growing impatience of the Japanese was given when General Ando, commanding the Japanese forces in Canton, published an open letter challenging Chiang Kai-shek to a decisive engagement, characterizing the proposed plan of prolonged resistance as "contemptible and unworthy of the honor of a soldier" (*ibid.*, December 15, 1938).

After the fall of Hankow, Colonel Takahashi of the Japanese G.H.Q. frankly admitted that Japanese advance beyond Ichang would be rendered more difficult by (1) the loss of the Yangtze (in its gorges) as a line of communication, and (2) the great difficulty of the land alternative, owing to the rugged character of the mountain country. This tactical difficulty was one of the reasons why the Japanese resorted to unlimited bombing by air of the

sumed operations in the Yangtze Valley in March, 1939, after a six-months respite for the refueling of the military machine and the protection of dangerously extended lines of supply.

In modern warfare, victory depends on the superior mobilization of military and nonmilitary force. Superior military mobilization can insure success only in those limited phases of warfare where man power and fire power are decisive. Japan has held the predominance of military power almost without exception since July 7, 1937. Her smaller armies are better organized and better equipped; her naval power has been supremely effective in its double duty of blockading the China coast and convoying troops from the islands to the mainland; her superior airpower has dominated the third dimension. There are several weaknesses in the Japanese military organization: the number of trained reserves is not ideally large for a task of great magnitude, and military power must be divided between operations in China and the defense of the Manchukuo-Mongolian frontiers against the Soviet Union. The insistence of the Kwantung Army on the full defense of the Soviet frontier reflects the further political weakness implicit in the divided military councils in Tokyo. In the short view, these weaknesses do not affect Japan's predominance in military power over China, but over a longer period they may become crucial. Meanwhile, China holds a well-trained army of some 1,000,000 men, supplemented by another 2,000,000 men under arms, in readiness for the first

---

Szechuan region in the hope of shattering Chinese morale. The theories of General Douhet have been generally discredited by the warfare in Spain and China.

Steiner: China

cracking in Japan's front line. Behind that army stands the tremendous reserve man-power of China, a large part of it militarily trained by the incessant civil wars of the century or by exposure to military conditions since 1937. China's military strategy is to avoid the disintegration of this man-power by refusing to risk its use until time, working through the factors of war potential, swings the tide.

The national war potential is the global volume of the non-military elements in the national life which assist or supplement the military power in executing the grand plan of strategy.[2] War potential includes such varied elements as the psychological adaptability of the population to the exigencies of war, the utility of the economic resources, the forms of industrial organization, the area and topography of the land mass, the size, density, and distribution of the population, and the national system of transportation and communication. Under the conditions of modern totalitarian warfare, war potential looms larger than military power in the plan of grand strategy; this is particularly true in China, where military power is not opposed in decisive tests. China must then concentrate on the superior mobilization of her war potential, secure in the knowledge that success there will win her the ultimate victory. Toward that point, all the cumulative experiences of China converge; from that point, the future course of China will take its shape. In that sense, China's

[2] E. Banse, *Germany Prepares for War* (New York, 1934); Oualid, Montgelas, and Hosono, *in* Interparliamentary Union, *What Would be the Character of a New War?* (New York, 1933), pp. 118–179; H. Rohde, *Deutsche-französische Machtfactoren* (Berlin, 1932); Helle and Ache, *La défense nationale et ses conditions modernes* (Paris, 1932).

chances of winning the present war, and the effect of that war on life in China, are two coördinate aspects of the larger question of the future of China.

It must be emphasized that the Sino-Japanese War has been fought on nonpositional lines ever since the fall of Hankow. This minimizes Japan's military power, which cannot be brought to bear, and explains the shifting tactics of the Chinese. China has merely to keep the invader in motion on the fringes of his attack, while guerrilla forces simultaneously harrass the lines of communication and prevent the enemy from consolidating his grip. Guerrilla warfare is not an ideal tactic, but in China it has assumed a special form. There the guerrilla organizations attached to the Fourth (Fukien) and Eighth (Shensi-Shansi) Route Armies are composed of regular and irregular soldiers, conducting coördinated movements in accordance with a definite plan of operations directed by radio from field headquarters.[3] These systematic operations give guerrilla warfare a character quite different from that

---

[3] The activities of the Eighth Route Army are described in the following: J. M. Bertram, "With the Chinese Guerrillas," *Asia*, Vol. 38 (June and July, 1938), pp. 355–357 and 421–424; H. Hanson, "With the Fighting Reds Inside Japanese Lines," *ibid*. (August, 1938); E. F. Carlson, "The Unorthodox War Continues," *Amerasia*, Vol. 3 (March, 1939), pp. 12–15; N. Wales, *Inside Red China* (New York, 1939). For details concerning the Fourth Route Army, see E. Snow, "Han Ying's 'Lost' Red Army," *Asia*, Vol. 39 (April, 1939), pp. 203–205, and "China's New Fourth Army," *ibid*. (May, 1939), pp. 257–260.

After the fall of Canton, the southern provinces were immediately organized on a guerrilla footing. Kwangtung was divided into 22 guerrilla *k'iu* (districts), while Kwangsi was divided into 12 *k'iu*. Chiang Kai-shek, with Yu Han-mow as second-in-command, took personal charge of the Fourth Military Zone of the southern provinces, replacing Ho Ying-chin, the minister of war.—*Sun huan jih pao* (Hongkong), December 4 and 23, 1938.

generally implied in the term. Such guerrilla operations succeed by surprise and maneuver, under conditions requiring nothing more than small arms, and their success is disproportionate to their cost in men and money. The demands for *matériel* are slight, and no heavy drain is laid on the national resources. Were China to fight Japan with Japan's weapons and tactics, the weakness in her lines of communication with the outside world would prove disastrous. But so long as China is set for the long war of permanent and continuous resistance, she may be almost completely isolated and still draw from her own soil, internal resources, capital, and population the sustenance of successful resistance. On further examination, China's war potential will be found extremely well adapted to this type of strategy, with its modest military requirements.

In the first place, China fights in her own bailiwick, utilizing the very vastness of her domain as an effective instrument of war.[4] Japan is drawn onward into a highly absorptive terrain, where man is puny beside snow-clad mountain ranges, mighty rivers, deep gorges, and enormous distances, and where the progress of a single day only serves to remind of the vastness of the task remaining. Until now, Japan has advanced through level plains at low altitudes. Rougher going lies ahead. Meanwhile, area not only fights for China's armies, but also gives to the new China emerging in the western hinterland a time factor of safety during which to fashion the instruments of defense which were lacking in 1937.

[4] W. Schenke, "Der Raum als Waffe," *Zeitschrift für Geopolitik*, Vol. 15 (September, 1938), pp. 705–711.

In the second place, the Nationalist government still has at its direct disposal a tremendous man power. The normal population of the regions into which the Japanese have not yet penetrated is approximately 225,000,000, but this population has been increased by the influx of refugees from the coastal provinces. To this man power at direct disposal must be added the countless millions of Chinese who would appear to be engulfed in the tide of the Japanese advance but who, in fact, have not actually been brought under submission. While direct Chinese rule has been extinguished in some 500 or 600 districts, the Japanese have consolidated their grip in no more than 80 or 100 districts. The available Chinese man power is sufficient for all military and economic tasks required by the generalissimo.

The raw-material resources of Nationalist China constitute a third element in the Chinese war potential. In the interior of China there is an abundance of foodstuffs—rice, wheat, and livestock. There is also an unlimited, if largely undeveloped, wealth of industrial raw materials, extending through a long list and including coal, iron, gold, silver, copper, tin, mercury, tungsten, manganese, saltpeter, sulphur, zinc, and antimony. Reliable reports indicate that much has been done to develop these resources within the past year.[5] So long as China continues her present tactics, no great diversification of resources or great quantity of any one of them is needed to maintain life, to manufacture small arms, and to keep a fighting organ-

---

[5] The survey of economic resources was contained in the Report of the National Resources Commission of the newly created Ministry of Economic Affairs (*Kong chang jih pao* [Hongkong], November 18, 1938). Notes on Chinese economic developments regularly appear in *Far Eastern Survey*.

ization together. The raw-material requirements of China would be far greater if China had to produce heavy artillery, tanks and tractors, and other modern implements. The importance of guerrilla and nonpositional tactics is that they place less strain on raw-material reserves and add to the life of China's resistance.

The form of China's economic organization is the remaining essential element of the war potential. China's economy is essentially rural and decentralized. Unlike Japan, she has no great concentration of capital and industry, and she cannot finance heavy war industries on the basis of a foreign trade in consumers' goods. China is divided into more or less self-contained economic areas, so balanced that the loss of a large number of them does not affect the possibility of continuing life in the remaining areas on substantially the prewar level. Chinese craftsmanship has its regional and local centers. The capture by Japan of the seaboard cities where the more modern industrialization of China took place does not affect the traditional craft economy of the Chinese interior. Throughout the present war the Chinese economic system has remained fully alive for all practical purposes.

Two new elements have entered the economic picture since the beginning of the war. Throughout Nationalist China, hundreds of new industrial coöperatives have been formed to exploit the natural resources and to manufacture finished products.[6] This development of industrial coöperatives, a

---
[6] "China's Industrial Coöperatives," *Amerasia*, Vol. 3 (March, 1939), pp. 37–42; P. S. Buck, "Free China Gets to Work," *Asia*, Vol. 39 (April, 1939), pp. 199–200.

The Renaissance of Asia

movement which is only in its initial stages, will have tremendous importance for the future economic position of China in world terms. The other new economic element has been the migration of Chinese capital into the interior.[7] China has had an immense wealth of available investment capital, the product of generations of exploitation by landowners, bankers, and other proprietors. Aware that the Japanese will confiscate or sequester the wealth of the occupied regions, Chinese capitalists have found it to their advantage to invest in the new industrial coöperatives. The profit is not great and the risk is high, but there is an opportunity for profit which no longer exists in the seaboard provinces. On this point, patriotism coincides with financial interest of the most selfish character, and Nationalist China is drawing the advantage at the moment. Overseas Chinese have also increased the supply of capital by increasing their remittances to Nationalist China. The transformation of Chinese economy and the availability of capital improve China's opportunities for success in the present war, while also laying the foundation of an industrialized Chinese economy for the future.

To produce necessary results, these tangible elements of the Chinese war potential must be reinforced by a spirit of Chinese nationalism. Something more than mere man power, land, resources, and flexible economy is needed if the war of attrition is to continue over a period of years, if China is to keep the principles of her long-range strategy alive in moments of military defeat, if her people are to accommodate themselves to the awkwardness of the situation, and if resi-

---

[7] *Finance and Commerce* (Shanghai), November 1, 1938.

Steiner: China

dents in occupied areas are to lend continual support to Chungking by constantly resisting the Japanese. In Europe, national unity, national patriotism, and national will are largely taken for granted. China has had a different kind of problem. China has been a linguistic and cultural unit for centuries, and minimum values of an ethical and moral character have generally prevailed, enabling social intercourse to take place between peoples of different provinces and different stations of life. In such ground as this, political unity might well have taken root. In China, however, cultural and social unity was so great that the formal expression of political unity became an unnecessary luxury. As a people, the Chinese were not politically conscious of the tie that bound them together while distinguishing them politically from non-Chinese. It is crucial to discover whether national political unity has been developed in recent years to the point where the Chinese might be expected to uphold a common political front against Japan.

In the ten years after 1927, the Nationalist government did much to create a China quite different in spirit from the China of earlier centuries. The process of education gradually framed the growing Chinese mind within a nationalistic ideology. Steadily the progress of communications, by wire, rail, and air, facilitated central control of movements between the different parts of China. Steadily the war lords of the northern, southern, and western provinces were forced to acknowledge the growing authority of the government of Chiang Kai-shek. Steadily there grew a popular insistence on operations against the Japanese, an insistence fostered in different

156 The Renaissance of Asia

ways by the Kuomintang of Chiang Kai-shek and the Communist government of Mao Tse-tung and Chu Teh. This rapidly maturing sense of political unity was nearing its climax when the Lukouchiao incident occurred on July 7, 1937. Have later events prevented that unity from attaining its full growth, or have they still further crystallized it? If daily reports from China, if the increasing difficulties of the Japanese, and if the constant hope of the Chinese have any meaning, then national unity has been fully consolidated. Conceivably it may be weakened by an extended period of social or economic stress; conceivably it may be weakened by political treachery in high places; conceivably it may be weakened if Japan is aided by formidable allies, creating a discouraging preponderance of power. But on the present record the political nationalism of China appears to be a deep-felt popular sentiment of such all-pervading scope and power that not even treacherous leaders can prevent the attainment of all that popular national sentiment demands.[8]

How effective this national political unity is may be illustrated in many ways, but perhaps best by referring to the construction of the Burma highway, which utilized some 120,000 local workers and large amounts of local capital. As recently as a decade ago the fiat of Nanking ordering the con-

---

[8] The pro-Japanese faction of the Kuomintang was thoroughly discredited with the expulsion of Wang Ching-wei from the party in January, 1939. See H. Hanson, "Firebrands and Chinese Politics," *Amerasia*, Vol. 3 (April, 1939), pp. 78–82. Even the Chinese Moslems have remained loyal to the nationalist government. See O. Lattimore, "The Kimono and the Turban," *Asia*, Vol. 38 (May, 1938), pp. 273–275; L. Hoover, "China's Muslims Must Choose," *ibid*. (November, 1938), pp. 657–660, and "Chinese Muslims Are Tough," *ibid*. (December, 1938), pp. 719–724.

struction of a road would have been openly disregarded by local officials; in 1938, under most trying circumstances, immediate results were had. National power and direction have extended into untold fields of economic, social, and political activity. Without it, the scorched-earth policy—*tsiao t'ou*—could never have found popular acceptance. What this new spirit of discipline means for the future government of China requires no elaboration.

We might ask why China now achieves political unity when she failed to do so under Manchu and Mongol domination. China's earlier conquerors regarded the wealth of China's cultural and social heritage with a large measure of envy. Instead of destroying it, they sought to nourish and derive profit from it. They had no reason to regard assimilation as anything but a final victory. Under those conditions, resentful Chinese were content to wait patiently until the process of history had done its work. Meanwhile, they suffered no great inconvenience. Conquest did not destroy the cultural and social autonomy of the Chinese; life in the villages followed the same pattern, whether Mongol, Manchu, or Chinese ruled in Peking.

In these respects the Japanese conquest is different. Japan does not look up to Chinese civilization as a superior thing, even though she has borrowed greatly from it. Japan has not been without success in assimilating other peoples to her way of life. She is not conquering China for the privilege of being assimilated, but rather to make her own conceptions prevail throughout all East Asia. The "new order in China" is a logical product of Japan's sense of national superiority and is precisely in that respect different from any earlier situation. Institutions of village and social life are being directly and profoundly modified. Chinese in conquered areas can see before their eyes the reason for resisting an aggressor intent on the conquest of China for his own purposes. They are given a motive that never inspired them in the past.

There is a general, but mistaken, idea that China may ultimately win the war by assimilating the Japanese. Japan's policy in a conquered China would parallel Britain's policy in India. China would be spoils to be exploited. Despite the intensive propaganda centered around the theme of population pressure, there will be no mass migration of Japanese to China. The only Japanese in China will be soldiers, administrators, business agents, and other transients with no intention of taking up permanent residence. In the absence of a large resident population, the force of assimilation cannot work, particularly in the face of a definite Japanese policy designed to protect against it. This contingency is realized in some form by nearly every Chinese, and with that realization comes further appreciation of the need for immediate resistance.

The final emergence of this Chinese nationalism is the most significant product of the present war, even though it has prewar origins. It becomes the fundamental assumption underlying the future of China and supplies the guarantee that the China of the future must differ fundamentally from the China of the past.

Where does this appraisal of China's resistance against Japan leave us? Several general conclusions emerge: China cannot quickly defeat or expel Japan. Japan cannot quickly overcome all Chinese resistance. China cannot quickly win significant victories or recapture more than parts of areas already conquered. For possibly the next decade Japan may hold large parts of China. Meanwhile, conflict will continue on the periphery and behind the lines. For another decade, then, the normal historical processes will be suspended or disrupted; chaos and disorder will generally prevail. For the decade beginning in 1949 we may still have to consider three possibilities: an all-China China, an all-Japan China, and a China divided between Japan and China. The all-Japan China is simply a logical hypothesis. It may conceivably be realized for a short while, with the most severe repression of Chinese nationalism, at a cost to Japan that will make the recovery of her expenditures still less likely. But although states do not make a financial profit from imperialism, Japan might elect to retain a precarious hold for other reasons. If she does, she must inevitably face a national resurgence of the type that Britain faces in India, in which event a new independent China must emerge. If Japan holds only a part of divided China for some years to come, she is equally certain to face the effective military prowess of the new China forming in the western provinces, and to lose that much of her holdings. When the forces at work in China are considered in their totality, the prospect for Japan is a dismal one. Unless she forges strong ties with powerful allies she has no chance for ultimate victory, in whole or in part.[9]

[9] Useful information concerning the problems of contemporary China is obtainable in a large number of current publications: Lin Yutang, *My Country and My People* (rev. ed., New York, 1939), chap. x, pp. 349–421; T. C. Lin, "Reality Conquers in China," *Asia,* Vol. 38 (October, 1938), pp. 606

At this juncture, there remain for consideration two other essential aspects of the future of China. First, what role will the future China play on the general world stage, and second, what will life in the China of the future be like?

In the four hundred years since Portuguese and Dutch merchantmen first appeared in the Orient, relations between the East and West have passed through three phases. In terms of the East, these were the phases of subjection, assertion, and equality. In the subjection phase, which ran to the beginning of the 20th century, the Far East was either out of contact with the West or else the purely passive partner in an East-West relationship. To the West, the Orient was merely a wealthy field for exploitation, lacking the will to assert itself. The subjection phase ended in the 1890's, for at least two reasons. The concerted Western drive lost its momentum when the European states carried their struggle to maintain a European balance of power into the territory of China. More important were the generating forces of resistance to encroachment in both China and Japan. By 1899 Japan had succeeded in throwing off the unequal restrictions of the Perry and Harris treaties and their successors. China had also come to have a growing appreciation of the imminence of her partition and destruction. The Boxer movement was a

---

611; *Asia*, Vol. 38 (Special Section, February, 1938), pp. 123–143; H. F. MacNair, *The Real Conflict between China and Japan* (Chicago, 1938); E. A. Mowrer, *The Dragon Awakes* (New York, 1939); J. Bertram, *Unconquered* (New York, 1939). I have also consulted a letter from W. H. Donald to H. J. Timperley, dated Chungking, December 30, 1938 (44 pp., copy in my possession). Neutral observers have been amazingly unanimous in their belief in an ultimate Chinese victory.

Steiner: China 161

pointed warning to the West that the process of unresisted partition was at an end. Since the Boxer Protocol of 1901, no European power has taken territorial profit at the expense of China Proper.[10]

In the assertion phase which followed, the unrestrained impulses of the West were fully curbed and the East began to be mistress in its own house. The popular reaction against financial imperialism as demonstrated in the Hukuang Railway episode was the immediate cause of the Chinese revolution of 1911. The reorganization loan of 1913 was the last effective gesture of the six-power consortium. Japan was recognized as a great power when England admitted her into alliance in 1902, and she proved the merit of that recognition by defeating Russia in 1904–05. China and Japan were both represented at the Paris Conference—Japan as a great power, China as a minor power. If China had not had the success of Japan in swinging the tide her way, she had at least begun to assert an active personality. The chief obstacle was not raised by the Western powers, but by Japan—the Japan of the Twenty-one Demands and the Lansing-Ishii Agreement.

In the present equality phase of East-West relations, the Oriental states are taking positive action to preserve their own way of life. Their device has been to adopt certain Western methods designed to strengthen their political, social, and economic structures.[11] This is a phase of Westernization not

---
[10] This reserves Russia's gains in Outer Mongolia, Britain's in Tibet, and Japan's in Manchuria.

[11] These tactics were early counselled by Yoshida Shoin: see Iichiro Tokutomi, *The Life of Yoshida Shoin* (Coleman translation), *Transactions of the Asiatic Society of Japan*, Vol. 45 (1917), Pt. I, pp. 161–163.

imposed by the West, but consciously adopted by the East, with modifications. After a brief flirtation with Western liberalism, Japan rejected it as unsuited to the temper of her people and institutions. Sun Yat-sen laid the foundations of Western democracy in China, and even through a period of revolutionary and wartime dictatorship China looks to the democratic goal. Economically, Japan has made herself more than an equal of the West in some fields and markets; while China's industrial revolution, well under way in 1937, has moved with accelerated pace since hostilities began.

One element in the Westernization process has been the desire of the East to expel the West from the political position it had established there by default. During the ten years of its relatively peaceful existence the Nationalist government of China worked earnestly to eliminate customs inequalities, leased areas and concessions, and the system of extraterritorial rights—and was substantially successful. On some points full victory was won; on others, such as extraterritoriality, success was promised for the near future. If the West was reconciled to the loss of its privileges in China before the present conflict began, it must be the more prepared to accept their loss when the conflict closes, whether Japan or China be victor.[12] Full equality is inevitable, if it has not already arrived in substance. That result cannot be regretted. China made it palatable by using the procedures of negotiation and by granting the West nondiscriminatory privileges. On the other hand, Japan in China has used her force to create a monopoly in which she holds the advantage over both China and the West.

---

[12] N. Peffer, "The Future of the West in China," *Amerasia*, Vol. 3 (March, 1939), pp. 16–19.

In the struggle between East and West for mastery in the balance of world affairs, the position of the Far East is not weakened by the fact that Japan is currently extending her imperialistic sway over China. It merely brings closer the day when the East will become active on a broader world stage. A successful Japan, fortified with the resources and reserves of China, would possess the greatest empire in the world, with more than 500,000,000 persons under her authority. No other single land area, save possibly the United States and the Soviet Union, would be able to match her economic power. If the Japanese effort collapses, which seems more likely, the Empire of the Rising Sun may possibly go into seclusion while a new Phoenix arises from the ashes of China. A victorious China may find herself caught up in the grip of the forces she had to unleash to defeat Japan. Taking the bad with the good, there remains the very real possibility that China may embark on an imperialistic venture of her own. This great China of the future is bound to be a tough China—let there be no mistaking that. Once a nation has reversed the flow of historical forces by its sheer determination, and has been given years to luxuriate in the full strength of its power, it cannot be expected to relapse immediately into a quiescent state. What the West must do is to make effective a system of collective security in which the full autonomy and equality of East and West are mutually protected. An enlightened Western statesmanship must recognize the possibilities for the future and adapt its present attitude toward China to the end that when the war is finished China need bear no grievance against the West.

164   The Renaissance of Asia

The future of life in China bears a direct relation to the future of the Open Door. Under Chinese rule, China may well remain the land of the Open Door, receiving and protecting on terms of equality the capital and commerce of the Western nations. A different situation will prevail in those parts of China which fall under Japanese rule. The life of large numbers of Chinese must be affected by Japan's attitude toward Western trade. Beginning with Manchuria in 1931, the door was adroitly but effectively closed because the Japanese were on the scene with superior military power, and because their officials took charge of the administration of the tariffs of China. In Manchuria, and later in North China, Japanese imports were smuggled past the customs barriers of China without payment of duties, solely because Chinese officials were intimidated by Japanese military convoys. The various puppet regimes hurriedly set up in Peiping, Nanking, and Shanghai promptly enacted discriminatory tariffs, openly tailored to suit the needs of Japanese exporters. More recently, military urgency has been advanced as a justification for prohibiting Western trade. In replying on November 18, 1938, to the American protest of October 6, the Japanese government observed: "It is unavoidable that these military operations should occasionally present obstacles to giving full effect to our intention of respecting the rights and interests of American citizens."[13] But at the same time, military operations have done much to introduce Japanese goods into the very heart of the Yangtze Valley.

Behind the mask of polite diplomatic phraseology Japan has

---
[13] *Tokyo Gazette*, January, 1939, p. 39.

revealed her deeper purpose. On November 3, 1938, the Japanese government officially announced that Japan intended to establish a "new order in East Asia" which has "for its foundation a tripartite relationship of *mutual* aid and coördination between Japan, Manchukuo, and China in political, economic, cultural and other fields. . . . Japan is confident that other Powers will on their part correctly appreciate her aims and policy and adapt their attitude to the *new* conditions prevailing in East Asia."[14] On the same day, Premier Konoye declared: "Japan is in no way opposed to collaboration with foreign Powers, nor does she desire to impair their legitimate rights and interests. *If* the Powers, understanding her true motives, *will* formulate policies adapted to the *new* conditions, Japan will be glad to coöperate with them."[15] This is simply a way of demanding that Western powers recognize a new situation in which "mutual" Sino-Japanese coöperation confers on Japan the right to close the door. Another passage in the note of November 18 makes this clear: "It is the firm conviction of the Japanese Government that in face of the new situation, fast developing in East Asia, any attempt to apply to the conditions of today and tomorrow inapplicable ideas and principles of the past would neither contribute toward the establishment of a real peace in East Asia nor solve the immediate issues."[16] In another sphere, Munich has given us an example of what may be done in the name of "peace."
Full advantage has been taken of military occupation to

[14] *Ibid.*, December, 1938, p. 16.
[15] *Ibid.*, pp. 18–19.
[16] *Tokyo Gazette*, January, 1939, p. 39.

introduce more permanent measures. Currency manipulations in occupied China, artificially supporting the new Japanese currency in China, have been disastrous to Western traders. Throughout the whole realm of business activity—in import and export trade, transportation, currency, and investments—discriminatory Japanese interests have replaced Western interests. What is important is not that the West has lost its economic equality, but that occupied China has been rendered completely subservient to the needs of Japanese economy. This monopolistic exploitation nullifies the normal economic development of China, and it must necessarily have an intimate and depressing effect on the life of all Chinese under Japanese rule.

We may now turn our attention to unconquered China and to the occupied China which is sooner or later to be returned to Chinese control. It is possible to make only a summary statement of what the projection of present tendencies promises for the future in postwar China.

It is reasonable to expect a greater ethnic and political unity to develop out of the present ideology of nationalism. The local and regional differences of the past will be minimized, even though this is a mixed blessing. National political unity also makes it likely that China will be governed by the strong hand—at least until conditions are ripe for full political democracy. The war has vindicated the statesmanlike stature of Generalissimo Chiang Kai-shek, and his must be the strongest voice for some time to come.

The destruction of physical property during the present hostilities affords China an opportunity to reconstruct her devastated areas along modern lines. Her industrial plant will be completely renovated and modernized. Intelligent direction of the reconstruction should improve public sanitation, better housing conditions, and in general advance the living standards of the masses.

Large-scale social and political planning will probably prevail in the new China. Ideologically, the social plan will be a compromise between the "livelihood principle" of the *San Min Chu I* of Dr. Sun Yat-sen and the rural reform program of the Chinese Communists. Chinese Communism, only distantly related to its Soviet cousin, will be useful in correcting the conservative tendencies of the gentry. There is, however, little probability that a general program of Communism on Soviet lines will take root. In a practical sense, Chinese planning will profit from the paper-scheming of the Kuomintang and the more successful planning of the wartime period. Large-scale planning naturally involves a new conception of effective national leadership in China, but a truly revolutionary shift in this direction is indicated by present events.

From these related premises, other consequences may be anticipated. Under war and postwar conditions there should be some elimination of present disparities in the distribution of wealth. Economically, China will doubtless be tempted to move in the direction of national self-sufficiency, unless there is first restored some degree of sanity to the general conduct of international economics. The new China will, in any event, undergo a rapid industrialization with a large measure of public control. The severe social dislocations which generally accompany rapid industrialization may be minimized by the

The Renaissance of Asia

traditional family and village organization and the inherent sanity of the Chinese.

This future of China will not be attained by unbroken progress. There will be inevitable reactions: the reaction of conservatives seeking to prevent the destruction of the traditional scheme of Chinese moral values; the reaction of capitalists more concerned with the prompt repayment of their wartime investments than with national welfare; and the reaction of other social groups whose loyalty to the national cause may suffer a loss of enthusiasm with the cessation of hostilities. While these reactions may break the pace of the postwar evolution, they can only briefly obstruct the long-range progress of the nation.

I should like to conclude with a summary of some perfectly obvious axioms. No matter who holds the reins of military and political power, China for generations to come must be peopled by Chinese. The Chinese people are today what the continuing and permanent elements in their social structure have made them. What they will be tomorrow depends on how that social structure survives the test of war. What life will be like in China tomorrow—the only thing that really counts—will be determined by the manner in which the war and the effort to win it remolds the social structure. Here China faces a crucial qualitative choice. To win the war, China must develop every helpful and advantageous element in her present social organization. At the same time she must be prepared to modify or eliminate those elements which work to her disadvantage. Her real task is to salvage from the war China's great contributions to the civilization of the world: her benevolent philosophy, her enlightened pacifism, her rich culture, and her inherent democracy. This is the quintessence of the whole problem of China. If to win the war she must sacrifice all that China has been, the world will be only mildly concerned with her fate. But let her pull through the ordeal of this war the revivified and enriched essence of China and she will place the world in her debt.

www.ingramcontent.com/pod-product-compliance
Lightning Source LLC
Chambersburg PA
CBHW070208250426
43668CB00049B/2103